Praise for *UnStuck*

"Stephanie Stuckey's book is an inspirational story about the rebirth of an iconic American brand and is a must-read for aspiring entrepreneurs on what it takes to build a business. And this is even more challenging for Stephanie because this isn't just any company; it's her family's legacy. Her story highlights the perilous path and the many highs and lows on the journey to eventual success. And every chapter will make you crave a pecan roll more and more."

—Jeff Perkins, Chief Marketing Officer, Greenlight Guru, and Author, *How Not to Suck at Marketing*

"Inspiring and authentic! *UnStuck* is a great read and a journey through southern American business culture—and a shot at the rebirth of a genuine American Treasure. Stephanie is brave, fun, quirky, and whip smart, and I was rooting for her before I read this. Now I know she's going to get this done! I remember stopping at a Stuckey's in a Country Squire, just like the one on the cover, and Stephanie's story does justice to both what Stuckey's was, and what she is making it, through her creativity, charm, and strong, southern will."

—Pat Egan, CEO, See's Candy

"As a kid on road trips, I ALWAYS wanted to stop at Stuckey's but never once got to—and thus I feel partially responsible for the decline of this legendary roadside chain. But now, I'm loving its return to prominence (and deliciousness) under the leadership of the talented and innovative Stephanie Stuckey! This tale of rebirth and revival is as sweet and fun as a Stuckey's pecan log roll—and it won't make your fingers nearly as sticky. (Not a guarantee)."

—Bill Oakley, former Television Writer and Producer, *The Simpsons*, and Fast-Food Critic

UnStuck

Rebirth of an American Icon

STEPHANIE STUCKEY

Matt Holt Books
An Imprint of BenBella Books, Inc.
Dallas, TX

Matt Holt is an imprint of BenBella Books, Inc.
10440 N. Central Expressway, Suite 800
Dallas, TX 75231
benbellabooks.com
Send feedback to feedback@benbellabooks.com

BenBella and *Matt Holt* are federally registered trademarks.

Printed in the United States of America
10 9 8 7 6 5 4 3 2 1

Library of Congress Control Number: 2023038336
ISBN 9781637744789 (hardcover)
ISBN 9781637744796 (electronic)

Editing by Katie Dickman
Copyediting by Michael Fedison
Proofreading by Ashley Casteel and Denise Pangia
Text design and composition by Jordan Koluch
Cover design by Brigid Pearson
Cover image © Pixabay / vicnutz / 212
Printed by Lake Book Manufacturing

This book is dedicated to John King
and to all the other John Kings
who created wealth for others without recognition.

This book is a memoir. It is my interpretation of what happened. I have revised some details in the interest of weaving a narrative and have changed some names to protect identities. The story is what matters. That is what is real.

Contents

Contents

Prologue

Picture this:

A lean-to shack on the side of a rural road beckons passersby to slow down to read the signs.

"Schley Pecans, 10 lbs for $1."

Another boasts, "Mixed Pecans, 10 lbs for 75 cents."

It's 1935 in Dodge County, Georgia, just below the "gnat line," as some folks describe this wide swath of land where the state's unofficial insect outnumbers people. The Great Depression has sucked the area of jobs, but pecans are plentiful. There's something about the red clay soil and just the right mix of sun and rain that produces more of this native nut here than anywhere else in the world.

Sylvester takes off his straw brimmed hat, wiping the sweat off his brow with a faded red bandana he keeps in his back pocket. The hum of a car engine approaching breaks the monotony. A sleek Cadillac, the color of lemon meringue, roars toward him.

"Let her stop, let her stop," he mouths, a silent mantra to a greater power.

His grandmother Cora Lee always warned him to save his prayers for big things; don't trouble God for the little stuff. In her mind, everything was little. But getting this fancy car to pull over seems awfully big to Sylvester. It's been a slow day, and he could use the money.

The car has Texas plates, the woman looks well cared for, some rich oilman's wife, headed to meet friends in Florida, he surmises. She slams on her brakes, stirring the air with rust-stained dust, her scarf keeping her tidy blonde hair in place. She gives the lanky stranger the once-over and surveys the pecan shed with its hand-drawn lettering.

"You must be crazy building a pecan shack next to a cotton patch ten miles from a dried-up town," she exclaims in a champagne bubbly voice before flicking out a cigarette with her manicured finger. But her gaze betrays that she's intrigued by the man. He's a hustler, just like her, only she hides it better under layers of makeup, perfume, and clothes. She buys ten pounds of pecans and throws in a five-cent tip before speeding off into the horizon.

Sylvester grins, jingling the coins in his pocket and looking off beyond the fields dotted with white cotton.

"I'm crazy, all right," he mutters with a tinge of bravado. "But that's what it's going to take to make it."

Chapter 1

LEMONADE STAND

Eighty-Two Years Later...

Y ou've never even run a lemonade stand. What makes you think you can run the family business?"

My father's words hung in the air like a *New Yorker* cartoon caption. Only I didn't have a witty retort like the ones that graced the magazine's pages. I pictured a blank bubble suspended above my head.

Dad was right. I hadn't run a lemonade stand. Or a business. Or anything other than grassroots political campaigns, PTA meetings, and environmental rallies. Nothing, it seemed at that moment, like a business.

I thought about my first career as a public defender, fresh out of law school. My clients were as tough as their chances of winning. "Facts are facts. You can't change them," my criminal law professor had taught me as a 1L at the University of Georgia School of Law. But—outside the confines of a classroom—I learned that you could change how you present them. The art of storytelling is what separated good lawyers from great ones. I spent my lunch breaks watching trials at the Fulton County Courthouse in Atlanta, Georgia. I was a legal groupie, my idols being famed litigators like Ed Garland and Bobby Lee Cook who could transform their often guilty clients into sympathetic victims of circumstance. I have always rooted for the underdog. And now I was one, struggling to defend myself.

My father's question lingered. I drew on the litigation skills I had learned watching those lawyers and trying my own cases twenty-five years ago. *Keep your anxiety and self-doubts in check and speak slowly. Words are powerful—they can sway others to convict or acquit. And when the judge asks you a tough question, pause.* The pause is uncomfortable, but it's also an incredible show of control. Like, *I've got this. I'm just waiting for my moment.*

Here, my father was the judge. And I was both the accused and the defender, with the facts seemingly against me. I did not have anything to say in my defense. So, I took the Fifth and remained silent.

I remembered the story I had heard about my grandfather, who I knew as "Bigdaddy." A rich lady in a Cadillac had called him crazy for selling pecans out in the middle of nowhere. Instead of feeling ridiculed, he was emboldened. People telling you that you can't do something is exactly what it takes to do it. Even if it is the people closest to you. Like

Bigdaddy, I had something to prove. That is what gave us our edge.

"I think this is what Bigdaddy would have wanted," I mustered. "Besides, there's no one else."

It was true. I had him at that. My grandfather had seven grandchildren, six of us still living. None of the others were interested in saving the family business. Number five of seven and the least likely candidate, I was the last and only hope.

How did I get here at age fifty-three, sitting in my dad's wood-paneled study getting a lecture like I was a teenager? It was such an improbable moment to be questioned about my professional competence after successful careers as a lawyer, state representative, nonprofit director, and head of sustainability for the City of Atlanta. Only two months earlier, I had been as settled and content as a tenured professor when the well-chartered course of my life was interrupted by the ring of a telephone.

———————

Pivotal moments, when everything changes, often come cloaked in the mundane. A knock at the door, a chance encounter, or—in my case—a call from the past.

"Hi, Stephanie," said a familiar voice. It was Greg Griffith, my dad's accountant and executor of his estate. "It's been a few years," he started, his tone as reassuring as it had been in my college years when Greg taught me how to balance a checkbook.

I cradled the phone against my shoulder, my earrings

dangling as I checked emails. "Everything OK?" I asked, reading through e-blasts about the latest climate-change news. He cleared his throat, choosing his words like he led his life—carefully and with deliberation. "Are you interested in buying Stuckey's?"

The *click click click* of my keyboard stopped. He had my attention.

"Your dad's partners and I . . . well, we're not getting any younger. And we're frankly out of fresh ideas," he stammered, going off script. But he picked up with a positive tone: "We think it's a good time to sell. Are you interested?"

Was I interested?

Stuckey's . . . the roadside oasis once known to generations of travelers along America's highways, their sloped roofs and brightly painted billboards beckoning weary drivers like a carny barker to pull over, pull over, pull over. My grandfather had built the business from nothing. He started with a roadside shack along Route 23, selling pecans and my grandmother's pralines, divinity, fudge, and the now iconic Stuckey's pecan log roll to passing motorists. At our peak, there had been 368 stores in forty states, stocked with confections made at the Stuckey's candy plant and delivered by a fleet of company-owned trucks, with billboards created in their sign shop. He'd created the first roadside retail chain. Before there was Wawa, Love's, or Buc-ee's, there was Stuckey's.

My grandfather built a vertically integrated business that dominated the nation's highways and was synonymous with the American road trip. It was a classic Horatio Alger tale, but—unlike some other entrepreneurs of his day, like Ray

Kroc and Harlan Sanders who brokered in burgers and buckets of fried chicken—he made his money selling snow globes, seashell wind chimes, smoking monkeys in fez hats, Mexican jumping beans, and wiener dog bookends. Most of all, he packaged up at an affordable price the dream that, even next to a cotton patch ten miles from a dried-up town, weary travelers could find a refuge of fun served up with pecan log rolls, pimento cheese sandwiches, and ice-cold Coca-Colas.

But that was then.

Bigdaddy had sold out to corporate America and became wealthier than a poor farm boy could ever imagine. He was proud of that, once boasting to my mother that he had made more money than her children could ever spend. Well, we had managed to spend it.

And, over the years, after decades of mismanagement by outside owners and heirs who ran through trust funds, all that remained of my grandfather's roadside empire was a handful of stores and family members with his name but not his business.

The thought of owning Stuckey's was a lot to process. On the one hand, who in their right mind would think it was a good idea to buy such a dumpster fire of a business? On the other, who in their right mind wouldn't embrace the chance to salvage their family name?

There was a lot at risk. Aside from the obvious of my being fiftyish with no MBA, I had recently divorced my husband of seventeen years. We shared custody of our two children, Robert and Beverly, ages seventeen and fifteen. I was a single mom; my oldest was setting his sights on college and my youngest was in private school. While I'd put aside some funds in educational 529 accounts, I had not amassed vast savings from my government and nonprofit jobs.

Oh, and there was the fact that I had zero experience running a company. I had never balanced a budget, other than my fourteen years in the Georgia legislature. Fighting over pork projects for your district isn't exactly a master's course in finance. I had spent the last decade doing do-gooder public service work on behalf of tree-hugging liberals. I thought EBITDA was a Swedish rock band. My relevant skills for this endeavor could maybe fill a thimble.

Still: Hell yeah, I was interested.

It was risky. It might cost my life's savings. It would literally be a detour off the highway of life I'd been traveling on for decades.

But an inner voice told me it just might be the thing that I was looking for.

"Ahem." Greg cleared his throat to break the uncomfortable silence, repeating his question more emphatically. "Stephanie? Are you interested?"

Breathe, one, two, three.

"Yes, I might be interested," I replied, trying to strike the right tone of cautious yet intrigued. No more checking emails. "Of course"—I cleared my throat while googling the various types of financial reports—"I'll need to see the balance sheets, sales projections, and P&L statements."

"Of course," Greg said quickly. "I'll send those right over."

Click.

I took a break from my workstation and walked around.

After recently leaving my job as the Director of Sustainability for the city of Atlanta, I was now leading the Sustainability Services team at Southface Institute, an environmental organization in Atlanta. It was one of those trendy open office spaces where upper-level management mingled with young associates. The pay was good by nonprofit standards, and I was doing meaningful work with people who gave a damn. Plus, they had a solar-powered building, compostable toilets, rain gardens, and bike racks lining the entrance. It had a very crunchy granola vibe, and I loved it. The break-room chatter (over fair-trade coffee) was on topics like vegan diets or the latest in carbon capture technology. We drank oat-milk lattes, wore Birkenstocks, and shopped local.

As I walked around, I wondered: Was I seriously considering giving up a life dedicated to saving the planet to sell pecan log rolls and rubber alligators to gas-guzzling tourists?

One thing I learned about being one of the few female representatives in the Georgia General Assembly (we were outnumbered five to one) is that you must find your inner well of confidence. I've never believed that I should "fake it 'til you make it." Instead, I prefer to "be real 'til you make it." Lead with authenticity—even when it exposes your flaws— and others will trust and ultimately respect you.

While it seemed like a seismic shift from environmental advocate to CEO of Stuckey's, it really wasn't. What really matters is being passionate about what you do. Whether I am saving the environment or my family's business, it is passion that drives motivation.

How often does a family lose their business and have the

chance to get it back? That almost never happens. Here was a chance to show that it could be done. I knew what I was going to do for one reason: I loved my grandfather.

I recall as a child walking the floor of the candy plant with Bigdaddy. He would introduce me to the ladies making brittle, greeting them each by name. I can still smell the burnt sugar as the ladies cooked caramel in copper kettles the size of bass drums. They would pour the molten confection on ice-cold marble tables. The brittle would shatter like pieces of amber glass. The ladies would sneak a warm taste to me with a shushing sound when Bigdaddy wasn't looking. Another memory is visiting the Stuckey's in Eastman, Georgia—Store #1—where they had a talking mynah bird that would greet customers with "My name is Corky, and I'm not for sale." I loved all the quirky novelties and pecan confections we sold, almost as much as I loved him. This self-made man who traded harnessing a mule for hawking candies and souvenirs was my hero.

That original store—like so many others—is now in disrepair, occupied by a flea market selling secondhand wares. The old Stuckey's candy plant next door, once bustling with activity and the whirr of machinery, sits heartbreakingly silent.

Although it wasn't free, I had been offered an incredible

gift: the chance to rewrite our story. Our narrative didn't have to end with our stores fading like scrapbook photos on the side of the road. My grandfather's legacy didn't have to be buried with him at the cemetery in Eastman, the Stuckey's logo on his headstone meaning nothing to passersby.

I thought about Robert and Beverly. This career move would lead to some lean financial years. Despite that, the question that persisted like a catchy pop song you can't get out of your head was this: "How would they feel if I let the family's business die?" And their children ... and their children's children?

I love *The Godfather*. But director Francis Ford Coppola got one thing wrong. With a family business, it's always personal and never strictly business. My decision was personal. I wanted to leave a legacy for my family beyond them pointing at fading blue roofs on highway exits, commenting to their children, "This used to be a Stuckey's store." My decision to buy Stuckey's was for my grandfather, whom I loved. But it was also for my children and their children. And for me, too, if I'm being completely honest.

It was also for the other family businesses that have lost their way, taken over by large corporations prioritizing balance sheets over brand value. When I think of family businesses, I think of Town Topic Hamburgers and its neon blinking sign—an anachronism in downtown Kansas City—and how it continues to fire up its grill day in and day out for generations of locals. I also think of Doumar's in Norfolk, Virginia, where the founder's grandchildren still serve up hundreds of ice creams daily on the world's first waffle-cone maker. Nobody casts an appreciative nod at the thousandth Dollar General store and comments, "Boy, that place brings back such memories." Yes, these chains offer discounts and convenience that we all need and enjoy. But the price you pay for the piled-high cheap T-shirts is a sense of community, belonging, and place.

Family businesses are the lifeblood of this country. I wanted to be part of something bigger than I or even my grandfather, part of an effort to put the "family" back in family business. When you have a calling that's bigger than you, you answer it.

So, instead of going back to my comfortable bubble of like-minded greenies, I ventured into the corporate world, trading my Birkenstocks for heels. Maybe I lacked an MBA, but I had something more important—a determination to change how our story ends. And, like my grandfather on that rural road in 1935, I was just crazy enough to do it.

———

I spent a few weeks reviewing the balance sheets and income statements and knew enough to know I needed help. I sought advice from several friends who worked in finance. The first two told me not to do it.

"Run, don't walk," away from this deal, is what they told me.

Which is why I sought out a third opinion. Not only does it make good business sense, but I finally got the answer I wanted.

"The financials are bad," my friend Paul Morris concluded, shaking his head after reviewing a thick sheath of Excel spreadsheets. Paul and I had become good friends when we worked together at the City of Atlanta. He had been CEO of the Atlanta BeltLine, the largest revitalization project in the city's history, and before that he was vice president of a $2.5 billion private equity firm. If he'd been charging for his time, the most I could afford would've been about five minutes. But Paul had graciously agreed to be my pro bono business coach in exchange for the occasional box of Stuckey's treats and some cold beers. As with most of what I was undertaking, I was punching way above my weight.

Paul looked at me sympathetically, taking off his glasses and rubbing the bridge of his nose as if the delay might ease the blow of the news. "But," he said in an upbeat tone, "there's something not on the books that should be accounted for." He looked me in the eye to make sure it sunk in. "The value of the brand."

Nowhere on the lines of profit and loss, detailing expenditures on salary, freight, inventory, and so on, was the goodwill that had been accruing interest for decades. All the families that grew up stopping at Stuckey's on their vacations to Florida in a woodie station wagon, begging their parents to pull over. The people whose expressions would change upon hearing my last name, exclaiming, "Stuckey?! Why, that's a name I haven't heard in a while. Good Lord, we used to love your stores and those pecan log rolls."

How do you monetize that?

I know there are formulas to calculate goodwill, but it's

a flawed exercise. Putting a value on precious memories that connect with a special time and place defies the rules of accounting.

That is what I was buying—not the sixty-eight franchise agreements that remained in place or the dusty merchandise in our rented warehouse, which, by the way, was the total of Stuckey's physical assets at the time. I was buying an emotional connection to our brand. And that was worth my life's savings.

Thanks to Paul's help, I was able to negotiate a lower price and put together the financing to acquire the remains of Stuckey's Corporation. The paperwork was drawn up, and a date was set for the signing and transfer of assets. Everything was in place, except for one final—yet critical—detail: making the pilgrimage to see my father.

My father is a man of contradictions, charming yet also difficult. To outsiders, he never sheds the persona of a Southern politician, quick to grace a podium with his oratory or liven a party with his war stories of being a congressman during the Lyndon Johnson and Watergate years. Even in his eighties, he remains a force with whom to be reckoned, still commanding attention like an emeritus judge. His nickname is "Possum," a moniker that pays tribute to his ability to elude adversaries and weave a fanciful tale.

There is a wonderfully warm side to my father, a side that loves his family and has worked hard to create a comfortable life for my mother, my four siblings, and me. But there's a toughness that strikes at unexpected moments, flipping from effusive to dismissive like a light switch. The unpredictability of his moods is something we've accepted as the price of admission to the Stuckey clan.

This is the part of family businesses that is painful to disclose—especially the pressures weighted on firstborn males that can result in addictions, estrangement, and worse. All things in perspective, we've fared better than many, but not without our share of emotional toil. This is not a tell-all confessional. I love and respect my father. But family dynamics drive the story of any family business. Omitting this would be like making log rolls without pecans. The strong personalities of founders and their heirs is a key ingredient in any family-business recipe.

Growing up as a Stuckey in Eastman, my father epitomized the big fish in a small-town pond. His personality was forged from being the only son and the heir apparent to the largest business in the county. He was groomed for that role, earning both law and business degrees from the University of Georgia and working as a vice president at Stuckey's for a decade after graduating.

Yet Dad left Stuckey's to pursue his own career, first in politics and later running one of the largest chains of Dairy Queen stores, along with other successful ventures. When he got the chance decades later to bring Stuckey's back into the family, I recall that it was with mixed emotions. There was a pride in the business that bore his name, but Dad had his own prosperous endeavors. I always thought that he lacked the passion for Stuckey's that he had for his other ventures. Perhaps because he couldn't claim Stuckey's as his own.

When I was negotiating the purchase of Stuckey's, my

discussion had largely been with Greg Griffith. It was his 49 percent ownership—along with several other equity share-holders—that I was acquiring. Dad remained in control of 51 percent and was not part of the initial deal. I knew better than to stray into the shark-infested waters of buying Dad out at this early stage.

With the price and terms for the 49 percent buyout set-tled, I trekked down to the resort island off the Georgia coast where my parents had retired. In a multimillion-dollar home overlooking the Sea Island marsh, my father remains as ac-tive and alert as ever, albeit from the comfort of his La-Z-Boy recliner. Up and reading the *Wall Street Journal* at 5 A M daily, fueled by a steady stream of coffee, he keeps a hand in run-ning the businesses he owns, including a community bank and timber company. A sharp gambler in his prime, Possum also occasionally rolls the financial dice on an emerging ven-ture with his friends and colleagues.

Unlike my mother, who devours Southern fiction by Flannery O'Connor and William Faulkner like popcorn at the movies, my father's oak-paneled library is lined with bi-ographies and self-help business books. In the evenings he'll pore over profit and loss statements with the same reverence as a monk reading the Bible. Growing up as his daughter, I always felt like this world of finance was an inner sanctum with a secret code I would never crack. I chose a more inviting path in law and politics, fields where I excelled, never think-ing I'd gain admittance to the mysterious realm of business.

The drive over the bridge—from the mainland, where all were welcome, to the exclusive enclave of Sea Island, where only credentialed cars were admitted—was analogous to the journey I was undertaking. In my secondhand Mercury Hybrid purchased on Craigslist, I felt every bit the outsider in the line of Mercedes and Porsches as I pulled past the security gate.

That fateful drive led me to the inevitable paternal lecture, detailing all the reasons why my decision to buy Stuckey's was foolhardy, which concluded with his cutting remark, "You've never even run a lemonade stand—what makes you think you can run Stuckey's?"

I had come to my parents' home seeking my father's blessings. While I didn't get what I came for, I left with something much more important: a gift from my mother.

My mother is the epitome of the Southern lady. She can be delicate and charming but has an inner resolve that helped her survive growing up without means in rural Georgia. With ivory skin, hazel-green eyes, and long black hair, Mom had looks that could rival the pinup girls of the day. She may have lacked money, but she was rich in beauty and talent. Mom won pageants as a teenager, tap-dancing her way into winning titles like "Miss Keep Dodge County Green" and "Miss Georgia Southern." All that grace and poise, coupled with a love of storytelling, captured the attention of my father, the most eligible bachelor in Dodge County. One day in 1962, my mother passed the Stuckey's in Eastman, on her way home from teaching English at the local high school. She made a U-turn, remembering that her aunt Bea loved pecan turtles. My father happened to be in the store that day, visiting his aunt Ruth, who ran the register. He saw my mom and was smitten.

Meeting the love of your life in a Stuckey's store doesn't work for everyone. But thank God it worked for Bill and Ethelynn Stuckey. Sixty years later, my mom remains the stalwart force behind my sometimes irascible father, the one who takes down his barriers and clears a path forward.

It was after the "lemonade stand" talk with my father that my mother, a model of grit and resilience, gave me hope when I needed it most. Walking out of Dad's office, where she had been patiently waiting within earshot, Mom held a gift for me.

"I have something for you," she said, handing over a box that was too large for her slender frame. She pointed to six boxes in all, the others stacked beside her. "These are your grandfather's papers. It's all we have left of Stuckey's. I think Bigdaddy would want you to have them."

They occupied the entirety of my matchbox of a car. Those time capsules of memorabilia would prove to be worth more than the corporate shares I was about to acquire. They were my lifeline to the past and my guidepost to the future.

With my car loaded down, I took to the open road, like my grandfather and my father before me, generations of road warriors who spent their lives on the interstate, measuring the passage of time by mile markers instead of the clock.

———

In less than a month from that first call, I set up an impromptu desk with a card table in the cluttered office in Silver Spring, Maryland. This is where the last two corporate employees rented workspace. This unassuming place was the headquarters of my grandfather's once-thriving empire. In his day, he'd had a state-of-the-art complex at 100 Candy Row in Eastman, the lobby greeting visitors with a mural of a pecan grove and a display case full of Stuckey's candy boxes. From the rows of C-suites with vice presidents in nappy suits and hats and secretarial pools abuzz with the clicking of typewriters to these two modest desks and boxes of files, Stuckey's was the poster child of a business in decline. It was a sobering moment. Nonetheless, I was grateful to the remaining employees who had managed to keep what was left of our accounts alive, shipping outsourced products from our rented warehouse in Eastman to our dwindling franchise locations.

I spread out the sales documents and managed wiring bank funds from my cell phone. Seated in that cramped room, with the stroke of a pen and the transfer of assets, I became the unlikely owner of Stuckey's Corporation. The documents required a CEO and—without one of record—I wrote my name down as the new company head with a bit of chutzpah. I was the unexpected CEO, a middle child who was never groomed for this. I thought of Bigdaddy at that first roadside stand as I signed my name. People can call us crazy, but that's what it's going to take to make it.

———

Reviving a business is different from founding one. Everything shifts with the passage of time. I realized I couldn't move Stuckey's forward without first understanding where we'd been.

While I plunged into the immediate task at hand of keeping Stuckey's operational, the boxes of my grandfather's papers stacked in the corner of my home office were like a neglected old friend. I felt guilty whenever I glanced in their direction.

After weeks of reviewing company files and trying to figure out how to dig out of our financial hole, I realized that the path to reviving Stuckey's was sitting in those boxes patiently waiting to be opened. I looked through the musty newspaper clippings, letters, photographs, company newsletters, and other memorabilia that the archives contained. They looked as if someone had hastily grabbed what documents could be found before the company ceased to be run by Mr. Stuckey. Whoever did this—I envisioned a secretary in horn-rimmed glasses and a cashmere sweater—would likely have never guessed that more than fifty years would pass before they would be discovered by Mr. Stuckey's fifth-in-line grandchild.

It took months for a cohesive picture to emerge, like waving a slow-developing Polaroid. It became my nightly ritual. I would finish the day's work, then settle into my next lesson on *How to Revive Your Family's Business*.

As I read them, "Bigdaddy," my warmhearted grandfather sporting cardigans and loafers, was transformed into "Stuckey," the self-made entrepreneur. His story gave me hope. He did not have a degree in finance. No one taught him how to manage people or run a manufacturing plant. But he figured it out. By reading his story, maybe I could too.

Bigdaddy's papers also contained a part of our history that was never talked about. I suspect that ours is not the only business with secrets locked in boxes—ghosts hoping someday to be revealed, like a message in a bottle eager to share its story after years of being lost at sea.

Chapter 2

PECANS FOR SALE

Nine generations of Stuckeys have called Middle Georgia home. Life was not easy in this region known for unrelenting heat and hard labor in the lumber mills. Originally hailing from Germany, my ancestors were of sturdy stock, their days dragging into years of felling loblolly pine and coaxing cotton out of the clay soil that left the roads looking bloodstained after heavy rains. When my grandfather Williamson "Sylvester" Stuckey Jr. entered this world on March 26, 1909, at the family home in Dodge County, his life's course was preordained. But my grandfather wanted more than this hardscrabble existence offered, a yearning that fueled resentment against his father, Ira. As a teenager, he spent his summers as a field hand. It was tedious work in the sticky humidity peculiar to the South—the kind of experience that either breaks your spirit or builds it.

My grandfather looked to education as his one-way ticket out of that life. He managed to get the money to attend the University of Georgia School of Law. He made it to his third and final year when cotton prices collapsed in 1931. Bigdaddy was summoned home to help save the family farm. Times were so rough that there was not enough feed for the family's mule. The poor animal would collapse from hunger and exhaustion. Bigdaddy would have to hoist him up to finish plowing the rows. Years later—when he was more successful than he had dared to imagine—my grandfather pointed to that moment as a defining one, like Scarlett O'Hara digging up a withered turnip to survive. Hoisting the mule was when he vowed to leave the family farm. If education was not his passport out, then maybe money would be.

It was the Great Depression. Jobs were scarce, but one thing was plentiful: pecans. The native trees grew wild throughout the countryside, and local farmers began to realize they could cultivate certain varieties to create a profitable market. Like other hardwoods, pecans are alternate bearing, meaning that plentiful crops are followed by bad ones. Good fortune in the guise of a hard-shelled nut smiled on my grandfather in 1931. It was a bumper-crop year, and pecans rained down from the trees like manna from heaven.

The pecans that were as common as gnats and humidity in Middle Georgia were my grandfather's salvation. It was a seemingly inconsequential moment that soon changed his life and his fortunes. Walking through town one day, he asked every shopkeeper if they had a job … any job. Bigdaddy was greeted with a sympathetic shake of the head by a feed and seed dealer named Bennett. The local shop owner did not have a job for him. But he had something that would prove to be better: a business idea.

"Why don't you buy pecans from the folks who've got trees in their yards, and I'll market them for you?" Bennett suggested encouragingly.

Buying and selling pecans was much more appealing than plowing fields with a half-starved mule. Like other Depression-era entrepreneurs who could not find a job, my grandfather did the next best thing: He created his own. Lacking the money to start a business, he begged his grandmother, Cora Lee Williamson, to help him. She loaned him $35. It was all the money she had, and she carefully monitored her investment. She insisted that Bigdaddy learn the pecan business as a condition of the loan. Cora Lee filled paper bags with samples of the different nut varieties for him to memorize. The bags were labeled with names full of history, place, and practicality—Pawnee, Schley, Cape Fear, Desirable, Papershell, Moneymaker, and more. Bigdaddy studied the intricacies of their shape, color, and texture and could soon identify which grades would fetch the highest prices. Backed by Cora Lee's money and tutelage, the twenty-one-year-old set off in a Model A Ford in search of pecans and a better life. This venture would one day span to over 350 stores in forty states and sell for the equivalent of $115 million in today's dollars. But in 1931, they were grateful if the car did not break down in the mud and pecans fetched a penny a pound.

That first season yielded enough profit for Bigdaddy to

open a bank account in town. But money was so tight that he had to hustle to make sure the checks he wrote did not bounce. As he would recount years later over jokes and martinis to big-city bankers, Bigdaddy had to resort to check kiting to make ends meet. He would make his rounds of pecan buying from local farmers after the bank closed since he did not have the funds to cover his purchases. Then he would rush to Mr. Bennett's first thing the next morning to get paid before the bank opened. Fortunately, fear of being arrested made him work even harder. My grandfather was never caught, and sales grew.

Bigdaddy soon realized that he could cut out the middleman and sell pecans directly to customers. Lacking the funds for a storefront in town, he built a wooden stand about the size of a chicken coop. With a sign advertising pecan varieties and prices, he was open for business. Sales were steady but far between. The moments of waiting gave him time to think.

One day he had a brainstorm on the side of the road. Always one to act immediately on an idea, as if it might disappear into the humidity, Bigdaddy ran the mile to the farmhouse he shared with his young wife, Ethel. He interrupted her bridge game to announce that making pecan candies would be the way to boost sales. "Why don't you whip up a batch of pralines?" he implored her. My grandmother, who I called "Bigmama," looked up from her hand and cocked her head. Her big-boned frame matched her personality. Her towering presence allowed her to meet even the most intimidating of people as equals. Theirs was a union of love and respect. In an era when women were taught to be a demure presence behind their husbands, Bigmama stood shoulder-to-shoulder with her often impetuous man, the steady ballast to his swerving ship.

"I've never made candy in my life," my grandmother said matter-of-factly as she dealt her hand and took a draw of her cigarette and a swig of bourbon-laced tea. Bigdaddy kept his gaze until she could no longer dodge it. Resignedly, she crushed the butt in the overflowing ashtray and looked at her bridge partners, her sisters Hazel, Pearl, and Georgia Lee. "OK, girls," she said with a sigh, "let's see if we can make some candy for my husband." The sisters dutifully fired up the modest stove and started experimenting with sugar, egg whites, chocolate, and pecans. Their creations that first year stuck to the classics. The bridge club turned candy club cooked up batches of pralines, fudge, and divinity four times a day in Ethel's home kitchen. Bigdaddy's wooden shed was soon graced with a new placard that read, "Fresh Homemade Candy—Made Today."

The well-trod path from their home to the shack led to profitability. The young couple managed to sell $4,500 worth of pecan candies that year. They were on their way.

Chapter 3

ROADS SCHOLAR

Those hardscrabble years my grandfather spent selling pecans along a dirt highway represented a life as foreign to me as the trailer parks we passed when we drove home to Dodge County for the holidays.

I grew up in Washington, D.C. With my father being in Congress, I was surrounded by the children of diplomats, politicians, and military brass. The kid with the funny accent who said "y'all" and asked for sweet tea in the lunch line instead of milk, I was a curious anomaly. The principal at my grade school once summoned my mother to her office to complain about me calling my teachers "sir" and "ma'am" instead of by their first names. My mother was incensed. "Where we come from, we respect our elders," she declared before abruptly ending the meeting. She left, determined to keep our small-town ways and Southern manners intact.

It was a losing battle, but my parents fought it valiantly.

Frequent trips back home—or to "the district," as Dad called it—gave us an understanding of where we came from. But, while I love my Southern roots, I was fortunate to have grown up outside Eastman. In my hometown, the name Stuckey would have given me an inflated ego. There was no risk of that at the D.C. private school I attended, where the morning roster included names like Roosevelt, Heinz, and Kennedy.

There were only brief moments when I thought our family had any notoriety, like when I would send letters to my grandparents. As a seven-year-old, I only knew to write their name, city, and state on the envelopes. Miraculously, my letters addressed to "Mr. & Mrs. Stuckey; Eastman, GA" always made it to their destination. It wasn't until other letters similarly addressed came back returned that I realized everyone else's mail required a full address.

I also remember that visits to see my grandparents, even for a few days, always got a write-up in the *Times Journal Spotlight*, the local paper. I chalked it up to nothing newsworthy happening over there. But the reality is that the Stuckey family in the 1960s and '70s was always newsworthy in Eastman. When I would walk in the local five-and-dime or go to the movies, everyone knew who I was. It was a surreal experience, and one I am glad I had sparingly. As bifurcated as my childhood was, split like a country mouse / city mouse fairy tale between two worlds, I would not want it any other way. Growing up in D.C., I escaped the inevitable sense of entitlement that can plague the children of wealthy families in small towns. But my trips to Eastman gave me a sense of belonging that I never found in D.C., a city where everyone was from somewhere else. Having two homes gave me the ability to adapt easily to different settings, from the country club to the Kiwanis Club. I'm forever grateful for that experience, which has served me throughout my life.

I lived in D.C. through high school, graduating from an exclusive prep school in a name-dropping political world where being a Stuckey was as insignificant as yesterday's *Washington Post*. Being a middle child accentuated the feeling of having zero expectations pressed upon me. Unlike the eldest son, my brother Billy, I was free from the burden of being the firstborn—or a male.

Credit: Stuckey Family Photo

Backseat Freedom: Me with my two brothers, Scott (holding our dog, Cricket) and Jay, in a publicity still for my father's congressional campaign. We took so many road trips in that Country Squire Ford that the odometer maxed out and went back to all zeroes.

Nowhere was that sense of childhood freedom more real to me than on our frequent family road trips from D.C. to

Eastman on I-95. My three older siblings always jostled for the front seats of our Ford Country Squire station wagon with the stylish wooden panels. Any notion that we were a sophisticated bunch, though, was quickly dispelled by the top rack loaded with unmatching luggage battened down with bungee cords. The best feature of our boat of a car was undeniably the back seat. Beneath its flat surface hid the wondrous fold-up bench seats that to my childhood mind were a marvel of ingenuity. I happily ceded shotgun territory, hiding in the back with my baby brother, Jay, playing "Yes & Know" games with invisible ink or fill-in-the-blanks with Mad Libs. Jay and I thrived in the magical place known as "the way back." We would build our own cities with pillows, creating a sovereign realm just for us. We even made our own currency. In the lawless land of "the way back," Jay and I ruled supreme. I credit a lot of my survival skills to those family road trips, fighting for food and attention. My ability to tell stories can be traced to creating our own entertainment in a time when computer games and smartphones did not exist, blissfully watching the world roll by backward through a windshield.

People often ask me what it was like growing up a Stuckey. We were just like other families that grew up during the era of the road trip. The only difference was that we did not have to beg our parents to pull over at Stuckey's. We pulled over. Every time.

I remember what Stuckey's was like in the '70s, with the wall of candy leading to the restrooms and the seemingly endless array of curious novelties like Mexican jumping beans, dunking bird toys, and pet rocks. I loved the snack bar with the milkshakes and grilled cheese sandwiches, the sound of frying, and cooks yelling "order up." More than experiencing the candies, nuts, trinkets, smells, and noises was the pride in knowing that this sensory wonderland bore my family's name. That my grandfather, who gave generous bear hugs whenever I visited him, created this place from nothing, instilling in me a confidence that anything is achievable. I knew the struggles he overcame to build Stuckey's—it was part of our family lore—and his grit and passion are part of my DNA.

What I also inherited from Bigdaddy was a love of road trips. It only made sense that I would rely on that connection to our past as I charted the future course of Stuckey's.

———

Almost immediately after signing the ownership papers, I made plans to visit all sixty-eight remaining Stuckey's locations. My strategy was to meet with the owners and staff, talk to customers, and get a boots-on-the-ground understanding of our operations. I did not have the luxury of learning my family's business from the ground up, like other 3Gers who are groomed from birth to take over. They start in the stock room and work up the corporate ladder. I was making the third-generation journey backward. I was learning from the top down.

Although the stores were spread out over twenty states, the task seemed doable if I tackled the stores by region. With the Thanksgiving break approaching, I ambitiously set aside a week to cover Alabama, Mississippi, Arkansas, Texas, Louisiana, and Florida. I recruited my son, Robert, to share in the driving. Beverly had no interest in joining us for the ride, opting to spend the week on Sea Island with my folks instead. The long miles seemed insignificant to me, having grown up in a family that considered the highway a second home.

Mapping the route for our Stuckey's tour was tricky. The company had been operating without a centralized database. I had to sort through files of franchise agreements to locate names and addresses for the sixty-eight stores. This led to the unfortunate discovery that most of these agreements had expired years ago. We were running a franchise business without valid contracts.

The legal state of our affairs reinforced the challenges we faced with the stores. We had little control over them. Stuckey's Corporation did not own any of these stores. They were all independently owned and operated. Only thirteen of them were the traditional, blue-roofed Stuckey's from my grandfather's era. The others were a "store-within-a-store" hybrid model that had been built in the decades after his death. Without a strong franchise program in place, these smaller footprint stores were inconsistent with their branding and product mix. Some of them, frankly, were an embarrassment to the brand. We had few tools to fix the problems, though, with out-of-date agreements and two sales reps being our only resources. That was nowhere near what it would take to run a franchise operation.

The best way to handle challenges is to accept reality. I

had mentally prepared myself that the stores would be very different from the ones I had visited on my childhood road trips. Yet, I needed to see firsthand what they looked like before I could come up with a plan.

My Stuckey's tour had an inauspicious start, unfortunately. The day before I was to leave, one of the remaining original stores in Nelson, Missouri, burned to the ground in a grease fire. My first interaction with a store owner was not as I had envisioned, introducing myself as the new CEO with fresh ideas. Instead, I reached out to Abdul Quddus to express my sympathies. Mr. Quddus, I learned, was a self-made man. Born in Pakistan and now an American citizen, he had grown his business to a sizable chain of convenience stores, two of which were Stuckey's. He was undeterred by the fire and was already working with the insurance company to rebuild.

"The store will be back in a year," he pronounced optimistically as our talk concluded. While it was not what I had expected, that first conversation with a store owner was exactly what I needed: a hopeful spirit rising from the ashes.

A couple of weeks later, Robert and I set out on our journey, my reliable Mercury Milan stuffed to the gills with clothes and provisions. Stuckey's "Essential Rules of the Road" include packing clothes for any occasion and compiling a killer playlist with podcasts, tunes, and books. Robert, on the other hand, threw a few pairs of underwear and some T-shirts in a plastic bag and was ready. The one item we both packed was the most important—a sense of adventure. We left Atlanta in our rearview mirror, headed for Alabama in search of Stuckey's and what remained of our family legacy.

The first several days of our journey were a blend of the good and mediocre—but mostly mediocre. The bleak financials were a prelude on paper to what we saw in real life. More than a few of the stores were only just "cleanish," the Stuckey's displays half empty, and the overall experience lacking specialness. The candies and nuts were often stocked haphazardly, with handwritten signs—some even on Post-it Notes—offering sales prices and promotions. The falsa blankets were piled high and not terribly organized. My son was a trooper, although it was evident from his face that he was having doubts about my decision to sink my life's savings—and his inheritance—into this venture.

Most of the owners were absentee. A handful of locations were owned by large c-store chains; meeting them would entail a visit to a corporate headquarters in other states. The managers were sometimes available, often not. Establishing a relationship proved challenging, as the c-store industry is prone to turnover. The reps did their best to maintain a rapport with the local managers but were limited by the long distances and number of stores they had to service.

I remained in good spirits, though, and kicked off my social-media posts about the trip by announcing that I would visit all sixty-eight Stuckey's locations. A reporter with the *Atlanta Journal-Constitution* saw it and called me for an interview. Her article ran with the headline "Heiress Drives Family Legacy. Stuckey's on the Road to Revival." While I subscribe to the adage that "any publicity is good publicity,"

I shook my head at the "heiress" reference. When I think of an heiress, I picture Paris Hilton or Teresa Heinz Kerry, who inherited vast fortunes—not someone like me who sunk her life's savings into a floundering family business.

Heiress references aside, the article also set an ambitious goal for me. What I could have possibly dismissed as an over-zealous plan lost in a string of tweets was now memorialized in the most-read publication in Georgia. *Damn*, I thought. *Now I really have to visit all these stores.*

The bar set high, I started posting upbeat dispatches from the road. "Stopping in Marietta for some pecan log rolls and a giant Stuckey's pencil," read one from Oklahoma. The store needed some TLC, so I took a selfie a good distance from the entrance and held the souvenir pencil up close to the lens, drawing attention away from the peeling paint and fading logo. I watched YouTube videos on how to edit and use fil-ters to improve my photography skills. While still true to the stores' appearances, I learned to use unique angles and close-ups to make them more appealing. There were some stores that looked amazing and needed no photographic touch-ups, like the one in Summerton, South Carolina, which features a dog park, and in Johnston City, Illinois, which has a delight-ful statuary garden with a *Venus de Milo* replica. Overall, I was feeling positive about the store visits.

And then, about a week into our journey, I hit—like my grandfather—my mule-hoisting moment as Robert and I visited one of the original blue-roofed stores in Marion, Ar-kansas. The exit was tricky, with a confusing set of turns on a bypass road to get to the Stuckey's. In retrospect, it was like a veiled warning to turn back, as the place was about the sorriest sight I could imagine. Two of the four gas pumps were broken, with plastic bags placed over them. The roof had been painted a darker shade of blue than the Stuckey's trademark teal. As if in protest, the original color had begun to peek through in patches. The Stuckey's logo on the rooftop was coming loose at the edges, like a cheap decal on a skateboard that had been left in a garage for too long. To complete this sorry tableau was a gash on the right corner of the roof that looked like the store had lost a barroom brawl.

"Dear God," I whispered under my breath—low enough, I hoped, so my sleeping son wouldn't hear.

I sat there crying. All the stress of getting a divorce, becoming a single mom, leaving my secure job, and putting my finances at risk for a company operating on shaky legal ground hit me at that moment. I looked over at Robert and wondered what on earth I had done with my life. I resorted to a coping skill that has gotten me through the hardest times: intense focus on the present reality. If I can deal with what is happening right now and not stress about the future, I will be OK.

It worked. After a few minutes of staring out the windshield, I saw that what I needed was right in front of me: my dashboard Jesus. I had bought him as a lucky talisman for my trip, sticking the wobbly savior above my air-conditioning vent. On long stretches of road when the caffeine buzz was fading, I would rub his head and pray to stay awake. Maybe it was only a variety-store tchotchke, but my dashboard Jesus brought me comfort. I turned my phone camera lens to Jesus and snapped a close-up, his arms upstretched in a plea for deliverance. In the background, while the fading paint and torn roof were still visible, it was Jesus that took center stage, saying more than words could convey.

Credit: Holly Aguirre

My "Come to Jesus" moment in the parking lot
of a rundown Stuckey's.

Our comeback journey would need faith—and some divine intervention—to make it.

With the social-media post out of the way, I took a deep

breath and ventured inside. I had come all this way to Marion; I might as well get the full, raw experience. I braced myself for what I expected: cheap souvenirs on dusty shelves, stale coffee with powdered creamer, and video poker games in the corner. Instead, I was greeted with quite the opposite.

The store actually looked good on the inside. There was a nice array of Stuckey's products along the back candy wall. The bathroom was clean, the floors scrubbed, and the coffee hot and strong. My favorite was the merchandise. They had a fun selection of some of our classic kitsch: ashtrays shaped like toilets that said, "Put your butts here," redneck fly swatters, cowboy hats, and corncob pipes. I remembered what my father used to say when his high-society friends in D.C. would joke about our stores. "We ain't Neiman Marcus," Dad would shoot back in an exaggerated Southern drawl. "Stuckey's is 'Merica," deliberately dropping the "A" to emphasize his point. Our brand may be tacky at times, but we have never been pretentious. I have always loved that about Stuckey's.

I picked up a mug that read, "Mess with me and you mess with the whole trailer park" for my mug collection and got in line at the checkout. Yes, there was a line, and the doors swung open with regularity as locals came in for their morning cigarettes, coffee, and lottery tickets. I asked the man behind me why he stopped here when the store looked so bad outside.

"I love Stuckey's," he answered with a friendly smile. "I remember when they were *the* place to stop." He stopped and looked through the plate glass window at the roof. "Yeah, maybe this store is a fixer-upper, but so am I. And so is this country." I wish I had gotten his name, that anonymous man whose comment marked a turning point in my comeback journey and my life. I hope he reads this. If so, please know I am forever grateful.

Getting back in my car, I pulled up the financials for the store on my computer. They were encouraging. It was not our top-performing store, but it was consistently bringing in revenue, thanks to sales of our pecan log rolls, pecan snacks, divinity, pralines, and falsa blankets. Seeing the store's interior and its numbers started me thinking about how I could revive the company. Maybe we did not own or operate the stores. And maybe some of them had seen better days. But the brand still had value, and our products were selling. That realization was critical to reviving Stuckey's, although putting together a plan and team to make it happen would take years.

I cranked up the air-conditioning. Robert awoke with sweaty hair sticking to his forehead. He rubbed his eyes and stared at the store.

"What a dump!" he murmured in half-awake disbelief.

"I know, it's seen better days," I said, smiling at him, "But I'm more encouraged than ever that Stuckey's is going to make it."

"If you say so," he said, letting the "so" linger for effect.

I handed him the trailer-park mug that I had washed out and filled with coffee and a dash of cream, just the way he liked it. He laughed, reading the inscription.

"Yeah, OK, as long as we can laugh about it, I guess it's going to be all right."

As we drove off toward Texas, I thought about my grand-father's defining moment in the sweltering Georgia heat, de-termined to forge a better life. This was my "come to Jesus" moment. Literally. In the guise of a plastic dashboard savior, I found roadside salvation in the most unlikely of places. The fact that folks still pulled over for coffee and pecan log rolls told me more than any high-priced consultant ever could: That this brand had sticking power. Despite the sad condi-tion of some of our stores, we were built to last. The paint and logo might be fading, but the brand and the memories of what Stuckey's once was—and could be again—were still very much alive.

From that moment on, our road trip picked up, not only in miles traveled but in experiences. We visited several stores that would have lived up to my grandfather's standards, with owners and managers that cared about the brand. Like Russ and Candy Whiteside, the brother-and-sister team that ran the Stuckey's in Hattiesburg, Mississippi, who greet regulars and newcomers with warm smiles and the smell of freshly made fudge. The store is chock-full of merchandise, the shelves stocked with shell figurines, salt and pepper shakers, shot glasses, and snow globes.

Hattiesburg was in a close race with Anahuac, Texas, as our top-performing store in sales. The visit to Anahuac intro-duced me to a Pakistani immigrant turned American named Shabaz Raza, who everyone called "Raza." Brimming with energy, Raza walked me through a store that was triple the size of the original Stuckey's. His vision was to build larger travel plazas that catered to families and truckers alike, dozens of gleaming gas pumps outside, and rows of merchandise and food options inside. Amazingly, this man who did not grow up taking road trips on American highways and stopping at our stores had a stronger sense of excitement for our brand than most.

"I love this country, and I love all things American. Stuckey's is a great brand. We're going to make a lot of money," he said, proud to be living the entrepreneurial dream in his adopted home.

The trip also became more interesting as I learned to find the hidden treasures in the small towns we visited. When I first embarked, I would stick to the highways to make good time, neglecting the back roads that offered vistas of interesting buildings with rich histories or local coffee shops and breweries. But as I became more comfortable with the cadence of the trip, I spent my evenings plotting out unusual towns or attractions to explore along our route, researching where I could find things like the "world's largest brick." These places spoke to me in a personal way. Finding beauty in unexpected places was at the crux of our brand story. So, I began pulling over to explore the Southern Maid Donut shop in Shreveport, Louisiana, where Elvis used to eat, and the motel in Meridian, Mississippi, that had been designed by noted architect Chris Risher. One of my favorite stops was the quirky Oasis Travel Center in Robertsdale, Alabama, which features a Scooby-Doo-style van crashing into the front. Visiting these offbeat curiosities helped define my sense of purpose in reviving Stuckey's: to celebrate what's often unnoticed but bears incredible charm and perseverance.

Robert and I concluded our road trip by taking a southern route through the states we had earlier crossed. Throughout our journey, we encountered what I referred to as "ghost stores," former Stuckey's that were either converted to other businesses or, worse, completely shuttered. But as I had realized in Marion, our stores had good bones and were built to last. Many of them were repurposed for a variety of uses—from a motor home dealership to a quilt shop to even someone's home.

I had been sharing daily missives from our Stuckey's tour on social media but had yet to gain solid traction. With a few hundred followers—mostly from my legal, political, and sustainability years—I was lucky to garner a dozen likes per post. I had yet to find my voice. That began to change when I swerved off I-65 at a ghost Stuckey's in Alabama. By now, Robert was used to my frequent stops and bore it all gamely. I got out of the car at the run-down place and snapped a photo. Despite the building not having been a Stuckey's in over a decade, one of our yellow logo signs still stood out front.

Having already used my dashboard Jesus as a photo prop, I was out of creative ideas for making this store look presentable. It was not one of our franchised stores, so I decided to show the building as it was. I regularly received comments and messages about the poor condition of our stores. It made sense to tell the truth about our brand while still conveying hope. I posted a short caption as I hit the POST button from my iPhone that read, "Been driving the backroads of Alabama in search of lost Stuckey's, determined [to] reclaim & rebrand them. Like our country, Stuckey's is a fixer upper, but I'm ready to do everything I can to help heal and rebuild both."

Robert gave a quick blow of the horn, a not-so-subtle reminder that lunchtime was nearing. For the next few hours, as we journeyed toward Florida, my phone kept dinging with LinkedIn notices. I checked after about an hour, and the post had gotten hundreds of likes and views. Most importantly, it had generated real engagement with encouraging comments from folks sharing their memories of stopping at Stuckey's. I cut the notifications function off so I could focus on driving, but by that evening the post had gotten over a thousand likes and tens of thousands of views.

I was finding my voice. The entrepreneurial journey, I was realizing, is about being alone together. There are days when I feel isolated and anxious about the future, but I have found incredible comfort in the community of people who believe that comebacks are possible. That LinkedIn post from the back roads of Alabama was the moment I first knew I am not making this journey by myself. There are thankfully thousands of people along for the ride with me.

From that point forward, I gained confidence in sharing my story authentically. As we hit the last original Stuckey's on our route in Bagdad, Florida, I snapped photos and posted them. One customer sent me a message about how tacky that store looked, loaded up with merchandise hanging from the ceilings that were, as he wrote, "an assault to good taste and one's senses." My former people-pleasing self would have apologized. But as I began to connect more strongly with our brand, I not only responded that hanging stuff from the rafters is what Stuckey's is all about, but I also boasted about it in a post. I quoted one of my favorite books, *Made in America* by Sam Walton, about "hang 'em high, sell 'em cheap," and embraced the kitschy-ness of our brand.

I have learned to accept that not everyone is going to love your brand, a hard lesson when you have an emotional connection to a family business. But if you try too hard to attract every customer, you lose what makes you special. As a startup, the only way we can compete with the large corporations is to be unique and different. We will never beat them on value or price, but we can find our niche and be profitable.

I concluded that first road trip at my parents' home on Sea Island. My father and I were on good terms, but we steered clear of business discussions, which would've been too fraught with conflict. The week on the road with Robert taught me to find the beauty in unexpected places, to pay attention to the details, and find my own voice. Those lessons would serve me well as I continued my journey to revive Stuckey's.

Chapter 4

AMERICA'S NATIVE NUT

Without pecans, there would be no Stuckey's. The nut's history is as much a part of ours as Cora Lee's $35 loan. Our stories have unheralded heroes—Indigenous people, African Americans, women toiling in kitchens—who deserve to be acknowledged. This is my attempt to make it so.

Unlike other nuts we find on our grocery shelves—almonds, cashews, pistachios—the pecan is the only commercial nut native to our country. For centuries, pecan trees have grown feral from the banks of the Mississippi to West Texas fields. We also find them invading our city streets, courthouse lawns, and backyards across America, growing as effortlessly as weeds. Generations of families have gathered nuts from their lawns, hurrying to complete their task before the crop falls prey to hungry squirrels or pilfering neighbors. In the evenings, Americans have sat on front porches and cracked bowls of the hard-shelled nut, sharing stories and sneaking the occasional taste, saving the rest for holiday pies. This connection to place, to the fruits of the land, is as much a part of who we are as the surnames we bear.

Centuries before this front-porch sitting and my grandfather's bumper crop came the Native Americans, the first to discover pecans. Wandering tribes learned to coax—with some effort—the rich, buttery meat out of their shells, christening their tasty find *pacane*, the Algonquian word for "nut that's hard to crack." Pecans became a dietary staple of tribes along the lowlands of the Mississippi and its tributaries for generations.

They would take the plentiful food with them for sustenance on hunting excursions and introduced them to fur traders. It was through this chain of passage that pecans made their way to the home of George Washington, who planted pecans at Mount Vernon in 1775. Washington filled his pockets with them as a quick source of energy while fighting the Revolutionary War. Pecans are arguably as patriotic as apple pie. The carefully measured hundred-calorie bags found on grocery shelves today can trace their origins to the Father of Our Country, who stored handfuls of pecans in his pockets as a midday treat.

Even more significant than Washington is one of the least-known figures in the history of the pecan—a man remembered only by his first name, Antoine. A slave at Oak Alley Plantation, north of New Orleans in the 1840s, Antoine was a highly skilled gardener. He pioneered the use of grafting techniques to eventually cultivate 126 trees with desirable thin-shelled nuts. His techniques proved that the pecan crops that grew wild on soggy riverbanks could be harvested with consistent quality and yield.

After Antoine's death, Oak Alley had a succession of owners who cut down his experimental orchard in order to grow more profitable sugarcane crops. Thankfully, enough of his original cultivars remained for a subsequent owner, Hubert Bonzano, to display them at the Centennial Exhibition in Philadelphia in 1876. Antoine's pecans were a sensation, along with Alexander Graham Bell's telephone, the Remington typewriter, and Heinz ketchup. The prizewinning entry, dubbed the "Centennial," became the world's first designated pecan variety and was commended for its "remarkably large size, tenderness of shell, and very special excellence."

Other farmers began copying Antoine's methods, leading the way to superior breeds and broader propagation. Thus, it was thanks to a slave almost forgotten by time that the commercial pecan industry was born.

By the turn of the twentieth century, farmers across the South were planting new types of pecans as an alternative to King Cotton. The pecan market continued to expand until, by 1936, in Georgia alone, twenty million pounds were produced annually.

This is where the histories of my family and the pecan intersect. Sylvester Stuckey, working in the cotton fields, witnessed firsthand the growth of the pecan industry. The pecan, being natural and plentiful, represented opportunity that led to the roadside stand. After the interruption of my grandmother's bridge game, pecans and her kitchen became the epicenter of the Stuckey's universe.

Ethel's first confection was a staple of Junior League cookbooks and church-covered dish suppers: the praline. A heavenly combination of sugar, corn syrup, milk, butter, and chopped nuts, its history—like that of the pecan—is deeply rooted in the history of the South. Originating in France and Belgium and featuring almonds and cocoa, French settlers brought the recipe to Louisiana in the nineteenth century. After the Civil War, emancipated Black women substituted almonds for pecans that were native to the region, thickened the mixture with cream, and the Americanized praline was born. A homespun variation of the French Quarter delicacy was recreated by my Bigmama, eager to please her enterprising husband.

Having mastered the praline, my grandmother advanced to the candy that awarded ultimate bragging rights for every Southern cook: divinity. The meringue-based treat gets its name from being so billowy light and sweet that it's . . . well, divine. Yet it is as unholy as the devil for its unforgiving demands on the novice chef. Although dating back to the early 1900s, the modern version of divinity is believed to have been invented by corn-syrup manufacturers to induce housewives to substitute their product for sugar. This is also how the pecan pie came to grace America's tables at Thanksgiving—popularized as an easy-to-make recipe on the label of Karo syrup. By contrast, the only thing simple about divinity is its ingredients. Consisting only of a few staples—sugar, corn syrup, water, egg whites, vanilla, a pinch of sugar, and, of course, pecans—it's one of the most difficult recipes to make, no doubt exhausting my grandmother's limited culinary skills. The first three ingredients are boiled together until they reach a hard ball stage, at which point the stiffened egg whites are very slowly added in a steady stream. Then the vanilla, pinch of salt, and pecans are added for texture and flavor. The tricky part is knowing just the right moment to pour the batter into the pan to set. And then there's the weather—a factor that must have led Bigmama to curse at the sky on rainy days. If there's too much humidity in the air, the temperamental candy won't dry properly, absorbing the moisture and turning into a gooey mess. It became a family legend how all her failed batches were thrown out to the hogs, later producing what my grandfather proclaimed to be "the sweetest bacon ever."

It was around the time Bigmama was perfecting divinity that she began to tinker with an old family recipe of white molasses, powdered sugar, and roasted pecans. After repeated trials—and further fattening of swine—the pecan log roll was born. Her creation, later eulogized by the *Florida Times-Union* to be "as sweet as a Sunday morning hymn," was a delicate blend of nougat and maraschino cherries, dipped in caramel and rolled in freshly roasted pecans. Her secret ingredient was the maraschino cherry—finely chopped and dried to prevent bleeding into the nougat—which lent a surprising tartness to the flavor. Ethel's log roll was a hit, and word spread that Sylvester's roadside stand offered more than pecans. The path to Ethel's kitchen was soon traveled several times a day to keep up with the demand for her delightful concoction. Long before Ray Kroc and McDonald's introduced the Big Mac, Colonel Sanders the bucket of chicken, or Dave Thomas the Wendy's Frosty, Stuckey's had its pecan log roll. Like those other restaurant chain pioneers, my grandfather realized the value of a signature product. And, to this day, the pecan log roll continues to deliver for us in sales and brand recognition. Even the Wikipedia entry for "pecan log roll" describes it as "a confectionary popularized by the roadside convenience store, Stuckey's."

Whether Ethel's pecan log roll was the first or not, Stuckey's can lay claim to making it part of America's cultural lexicon. The week I bought Stuckey's—after decades of our brand losing market share—it gave me hope to watch John Goodman joke with Seth Meyers on the *Late Night* show about pulling over at Stuckey's for a log roll on a road trip. Even with the passage of decades, Bigmama's creation is still our calling card—and a source of comedians' jokes. Our family fortune may have been reduced to dusty merchandise in a rented warehouse, but that comment by Goodman restored my faith that Stuckey's had sticking power. I may not have inherited millions, but I can lay claim to my family's piece of roadside Americana. I am not a conventional heiress like Paris Hilton, yet I feel rich beyond measure with my pecan log roll fortune.

Chapter 5

THE ART OF THE PIVOT

Sometimes when you buy a business, you are buying trouble. There is usually a reason why it is for sale, and that reason is rarely because it is wildly profitable or well run. When I returned to work after my Thanksgiving tour of the stores with Robert, I hunkered down to dealing with the myriad of problems the business faced.

At the time, all of the Stuckey's treats were made by outside manufacturers—even our log rolls. We supplemented our limited offerings with other nostalgic candies like Goo Goo Clusters and Gold Miner Gum that were stocked in Stuckey's display boxes. In our prime, Stuckey's made dozens of varieties of confections, from pecan puffs to rum-filled coconut Zombies, that filled a whole display wall. It would have broken my grandfather's heart to see that we had resorted to outside vendors to supply our product line.

While the team we had in place did the best with what we

had, finances were limited. Our merchandise line was often made up of cheap closeout inventory that we could afford on our meager budget. As a result, there was no cohesiveness to what we sold—unlike in my grandfather's day, when items were as carefully chosen as words in a story.

This business model did manage to keep us afloat, albeit often running off of a negative balance sheet. The warehouse distributed the outsourced candies and novelties to the franchised stores that were serviced by a local trucking company that ran weekly routes. Our sales reps visited each location monthly to check on inventory and fill orders. Had there been more Stuckey's stores in operation and a greater volume of products sold, this distribution model would have worked. It had, in fact, been profitable in prior years when the store count exceeded 150. By 2020, the franchise number had sunk so low that the company was treading water. The team all worked hard to stay afloat, but we were sinking.

On top of our financial woes, there were legal ones. I had to dip further into my savings to hire an attorney to deal with our out-of-date franchise agreements. While I had practiced law for decades, I adhere to the adage that the lawyer who represents herself has a fool for a client. Not only is that sound legal advice, but I also lacked an understanding of—or the patience for—the minutiae of franchise law. I retained a former in-house counsel of a national restaurant chain who had just embarked on a private practice.

After reviewing the documents I had scanned and emailed him, my lawyer called me. "Good news," he announced, front-ending what he was about to say with a positive note.

"You're totally in compliance with the law . . ." He hung onto the final syllable. "But you're in compliance with licensing law—not franchise law." In short, he explained, granting a license would allow stores to use the Stuckey's trademark for a fee. It would lack the complexity of a franchise program that required complicated governance. Licensing offered a simple solution to our legal quagmire. Simple, yes, but not without its setbacks. A license lacks control. Franchises like McDonald's and Dairy Queen have training programs, operations manuals, and inspections in place to ensure that their stores live up to quality standards. Stuckey's had only five employees, all of them stretched to capacity. This was hardly the makings of a well-run program. We lacked the infrastructure to run a banana stand, much less an interstate chain offering gas, food, and novelties. But thanks to our attorney, we had an unconventional yet legal path forward. I swallowed a dose of reality and accepted that we had to pivot to survive. After more than fifty years, Stuckey's would cease to operate as a franchise business. We would license stores moving forward.

Unfortunately, just as we cleared our legal hurdle, we were hit with a bigger challenge—one that was devastating to businesses everywhere. By March 1, 2020, the COVID-19 pandemic was in full force, resulting in mass shutdowns worldwide. Within only a few days, everything changed.

In moments of crisis, I've relied on my life's experiences. That is one of the many advantages of being a later-in-life entrepreneur. There's an emotional maturity that comes with age and experience that has proven invaluable in navigating hard times.

I was fortunate to have worked for the City of Atlanta as its first Chief Resilience Officer. My role was part of a global network run by the Rockefeller Foundation called 100 Resilient Cities. I had a wonderful mentor in that program, Otis Rolley, who now serves as president of the Wells Fargo Foundation. Otis and the Rockefeller team taught me what it means to be resilient. Resilience is more than bouncing back from a crisis. That's sustainability: merely maintaining the status quo. Resilience is bouncing back stronger. It is embracing that tough experience as an opportunity to become even better.

The Rockefeller program outlined two key components of resilience: shocks and stresses. Whether in the government, business, or civic realm, an entity must be able to withstand both. A shock is an acute, catastrophic event that impacts the ability to function, like a hurricane, political unrest, or a global pandemic. A stress, by contrast, is a chronic, ongoing vulnerability that tears at the underlying fabric of an organization, like supply-chain gaps, low employee morale, lack of diversity, and so on. While some shocks can be predicted, many cannot; thus, it is imperative to address the long-term stresses to be resilient. The saying "Don't let a good crisis go to waste" applies here. While COVID-19 was a setback, it also offered an opportunity to focus on the long-term stresses. Resilience for Stuckey's meant dealing with the immediate issues of generating enough profit and cash flow to weather the shutdown period as well as tackling the more persistent stressors, like a redundant supply chain and an unstable workforce.

Stuckey's was fortunate to be considered an essential business by the government since our licensed stores offered gas on the interstate. Thus, our doors remained open throughout the COVID-19 shutdown. We are forever grateful to our mainstay customers, especially truckers, who continued to stop at Stuckey's during this and other tough times in our history.

Our in-store sales dipped, but we survived by ramping up our online presence and expanding distribution to more retail outlets. Both are longer-term strategies that we continue to pursue. The sales reps and I also picked up new hardware and grocery customers. These sales channels were ones that fared well during the pandemic and have remained reliable accounts.

I also put my government background to use, availing ourselves of COVID-19 benefits for small businesses. We received funds from the Paycheck Protection Program and the low-interest, deferred payment loan to recover from the economic disaster.

As we saw delays from our overseas vendors, we started to cultivate new relationships with American manufacturers to make our candy and snack nuts, as well as the novelties we sold. While the cost of goods was higher, we made up for the difference with lower shipping costs. Our purchase orders were filled much faster with domestic partners, with whom we fostered personal relationships. Best of all, we were able to market our products as "Made in the USA." We have kept these vendor relationships intact and, post-COVID, still source most of our products from American companies.

The main lesson I learned from COVID-19 is that Stuckey's was at a serious disadvantage by having our branded candies and nuts made by third parties. When a crisis hit, our co-packers understandably prioritized their own production demands over ours. We experienced backlogs and delays that would have been less of a shock if, like in my grandfather's day, we were more vertically integrated.

Fortunately, we weathered the COVID-19 crisis relatively unscathed. Our sales efforts along with PPP funding resulted in a positive balance sheet by June of 2020. It was only $10,000 and some change, but a profit is a profit. When you start in debt, getting in the black is worth a high five. I sent a copy of our financials to my father with a message that read, "Maybe I can't run a lemonade stand, but I can run Stuckey's." I added a smiley emoticon. Within an hour, I received a reply: "I'm proud of you. Love, Dad." That one sentence meant so much. While true validation comes from within, it was gratifying that my father, who had built several successful businesses, thought I was on the right track.

That short email ushered in a shift in our father–daughter dynamic. My father realized that I could make a profit. And, now that I stood in his shoes, I better understood what it takes to be a CEO. This mutual respect helped transition to my full buyout of the company. Even with this positive turn of events, there was still a power imbalance with Dad owning 51 percent. For me to run the company my way, he needed to let go.

Dad initially resisted. He had an emotional attachment to the company. There were weeks of fruitless conversations with him. I could hear Fox News blaring in the background while I tried to get my father to focus on something other than Tucker Carlson's latest rant. I could not get him to budge. Finally, I resorted to my secret weapon: my mother. She worked her subtle yet persistent skills, urging Dad to sell his shares and free me to run Stuckey's my way.

I drove down to Sea Island in a last-ditch effort—back to the oak-lined study that seemed less intimidating this go-round—to settle the matter. Armed with financial statements showing how the company was trending in the right direction, my arguments about my ability to run Stuckey's were unconvincing. The deciding moment was when I looked at him and said, "You can have a business partner, or you can have a daughter. But you can't have both." I left him to stew over that with a glass of Jack Daniel's. Within a few days, he relented. I got a call close to dawn one morning. "Your mother won't give me a moment of peace until I sell you my shares. Stuckey's is yours if you want it."

I wanted it and had the transfer paperwork drawn up by noon. I had to liquidate the few remaining assets I had other than my pension fund and college savings accounts. I hated to part with what was left of my "nest egg," but if I wanted to revive Stuckey's, I had to be all in. There's nothing half-ass about being an entrepreneur. I got what I had been pushing for: full ownership. It was time. So, I sold the last of my investments and bought out my father. Within a few days, I was the sole owner of my grandfather's company. The middle child, the least likely, I was the only one foolhardy enough to do this.

Driving back home to Atlanta after my meeting, I took a detour to visit one of the few remaining Stuckey's stores. The roof was a vibrant red instead of the classic teal my grandfather had chosen. The logo on the building's side was painted a garish yellow from a misguided '80s rebranding. Styrofoam cups and beer cans littered the oil-splattered asphalt. The place was an eyesore. What on earth was I thinking buying this company?

I sat in the car and ate my road-trip breakfast of choice—gas station coffee and a pecan log roll. Each bite contained memories of my childhood and more recent recollections as well. Every time I posted on social media or spoke to folks about my quest to revive Stuckey's, the inevitable comments were about how our snacks and candies were a cherished part of their family vacations. The sales data backed this up as more than anecdotal. That moment in a chilly parking lot led to a revelation like the one Bigdaddy had had on the side of a hot dusty road. It's the pecan treats that got the drivers to pull over. Eighty-five-plus years later, we continue to make money from the sale of those same products. As the saying goes, "You dance with the one that brought you." Our dancing partner was—and still is—the pecan.

Pivoting our business model to focus on the sale of pecan snacks and candies instead of the licensed stores could be our path to profitability. Making that strategy a reality was the hard part. For that, I'd need help. I needed a team. More importantly, I needed a business partner.

Signs are everywhere. Not just blaring lights at intersections, but the more subtle ones that nudge you unexpectedly.

There are people and opportunities that enter your life at the perfect time. So it was with meeting R.G. Lamar Jr., who would join me in leading Stuckey's.

It was a good sign that I was introduced to R.G. while I was staying at our family farm in Eastman. A few weeks after I bought out my father, I decided to escape the city for the quiet comfort of the country. COVID had shut down Atlanta, and even my teenage kids were grateful for the freedom that acres of pecan trees in rural Georgia offered. This is where Bigdaddy would retreat to for solace and inspiration. Now, here I was, his granddaughter, two generations later, seeking the same.

I had developed a ritual of getting up early, brewing coffee, and sitting on the porch to watch the first rays of sun light up the grove. Leaning back in Bigdaddy's worn rocking chair one morning, I shut my eyes and traveled back in time. Pecan trees last for hundreds of years, so my grandfather would have walked through these same rows of Stuarts and Desirables that graced the orchard today. What was it like for him shaking the trees and scooping up fresh-thrown nuts from the ground without modern machinery? And if he were sitting here right now, what advice would he have for me?

The whirring of heavy machinery and grinding of wheels through mud interrupted my thoughts. A John Deere lumbered through the immaculately planted rows, lugging fertilizer behind it. A painted logo on the side read, "Lamar Pecan Company."

I realized how little I knew about pecans. Yet I wanted

to revive the company as a pecan brand. Maybe talking to whoever ran Lamar Pecans would be a good start.

I called Wade Hall, who ran my family's timber company and managed the farm. He picked up on the first ring, the sound of country music and a car engine in the background. I could tell he had been up for hours, likely out surveying property. I asked him to connect me with Lamar Pecans. "Your timing is perfect," Wade responded. "I was talking to R.G. Lamar yesterday, and he wants to meet you too. He has a potential business opportunity for Stuckey's." Definitely a sign. Wade gave me R.G.'s number, and I wrote it on the back of my hand, determined to call him before the ink wore off.

I poured a second cup of coffee and did some quick research. I found the company's website. Lamar Pecans had been started by John Lamar and his wife in the 1970s, then run by his son, Bob, and was now in the hands of Bob's son, R.G., and stepson, Grant. Theirs was one of the largest pecan farms in Georgia, producing over 2.5 million pounds of pecans annually. R.G. was active in the Georgia Pecan Commission, his name appearing in numerous online articles about pecan pricing and policy. He was definitely someone I needed to meet.

I checked the time. It was 7 AM, not too early for a farmer. I punched in the numbers. Like Wade, he picked up on the first ring, also up and busy with the workday. "R.G. Lamar," he answered with a hint of a drawl, like someone who had been raised in the South but, with years of absence, had shaved the edge off the deep twang. "It's Stephanie Stuckey," I said. "Wade suggested I give you a call." Within minutes, we were discussing R.G.'s effort to market the pecan as America's go-to snack nut. He had started his own brand, Front Porch Pecans, that was produced by a co-packer. Sales via Amazon and health food outlets had been encouraging, and he was looking to scale with manufacturing.

R.G. rattled off how he planned to dominate the pecan industry like a general mapping out an assault, only the territory he aimed to conquer was the aisles of grocery and convenience stores. He knew what he wanted and how to get it.

R.G. hesitated. The silence spoke volumes. He was thinking about whether I could be part of his plan. We each had what the other needed: a brand and business savvy. "I'm negotiating with some potential co-investors on a deal to buy a pecan manufacturing plant. It may be too late to bring in another partner, but if you're interested . . ." He let the question linger along with his doubt. "Well, I can ask them."

Overexuberance is best reserved for puppies and kids at Disney World. But I am not gifted with the art of subtlety. "Heck yes, I'm interested," I gushed before he had finished his last syllable. My hastiness contrasted with R.G.'s deliberate speech and approach, but maybe that would make for a balanced partnership. I sensed he had the steady temperament and mastery of detail that I lacked. I hung up feeling more hopeful than I had in months—yet also unsure I would be invited to join the clique of potential investors.

Finding the right business partner is like finding a life partner. If you don't choose wisely, it can be expensive and messy to undo. Too often, the focus is solely on experience and skill sets. However, emotional intelligence is even more critical. Does your partner have the stick-to-itiveness to withstand the highs and lows of running a company? Can you reach out in those panicked moments when you're anxious about meeting payroll and know there's a calming influence on the other line? Most of all, do they have a moral compass guided by the North Star of integrity? That is what matters most.

I spent the following days debating whether a partnership made sense. My grandfather had been a visionary-type CEO. He answered to no one and called the shots. He was a product of the Depression, with a go-it-alone mentality. The models of corporate governance have radically shifted since then. Today, some of the most successful corporations in the world—Microsoft, Airbnb, Berkshire Hathaway, Apple, Ben & Jerry's, and more—were founded as partnerships. Running a business can be isolating; it's less lonely if there is someone to share the risks and rewards—and provide honest feedback as an equal. The idea of having a partner was intriguing.

A few days later, the call came. The potential investors were willing to meet me. There were three young men in addition to R.G., all immersed in the pecan business since birth, like their fathers before them and their fathers before them. They were pecan royalty. They knew the varieties, the soil types, the ways to look at an orchard and tell if it would be a good crop or not. I was out of my league. I had only one thing going for me: a family name that had meant something in the pecan business. But that was fifty years ago. These men were a lot younger than me. They didn't grow up pestering their parents to pull over at Stuckey's. They didn't know a pecan log roll from a PayDay bar. My Gen X references to road trips in woodie station wagons would fall flat with these Millennials who grew up in the backseats of hi-tech SUVs with video games to entertain them. I did my best to dismiss these self-doubts. With a family business, you have to think in terms of generations, not quarters. The story of Stuckey's spans almost nine decades. Longevity like that isn't found on a balance sheet, but it's nonetheless worth millions. I just hoped the pecan mafia would agree.

The meeting went well over the hour we had scheduled, our conversation flowing easily. We had a mutual goal of advancing pecans beyond the produce section in grocery stores—claiming their rightful space on the snack aisle along with almonds, cashews, peanuts, and pistachios. We each had our own brand, so we were arguably competitors. Yet there was a genuineness in our shared passion for all things pecan. I liked them. They had been negotiating the purchase of Atwell Pecan, a shelling and manufacturing company in Wrens, Georgia, outside of Augusta. The plant produced a variety of snacks and candies, including pecan log rolls, pralines, and divinity. Aligning a brand like Stuckey's with a manufacturer like Atwell made sense, like one plus one equaling two—or maybe even a multiple of that if the merger proved profitable.

R.G. called afterwards to let me know I was in. I was elated. I had been offered a path forward with a solid team that, combined, had more than a hundred years of experience in the pecan business. Making this move would force me to let go of the stores as our profit driver and embrace a new business model. Sometimes the best way to honor the past is to move beyond it.

Unfortunately, though, the deal that seemed to be a "go" soon hit the brakes. The other potential partners pulled out. They had other profitable businesses and decided against overextending their resources, especially with the economic uncertainties that COVID-19 brought. "They're out," R.G. said resignedly. Then his mood shifted. "But I'm still in. Are you?" We had yet to agree on a valuation for Atwell Pecan Company, but the opening salvo was more than $6 million. That was a lot, especially for two people who had never brokered a business merger. But when options are limited, decisions are easier. Yes, I was in. There was no Plan B. The alphabet and choices ended here.

The following months were a blur of activity. We applied for a 7(a) loan from the Small Business Administration (SBA) to finance the acquisition. It was a lot of paperwork, even by government standards. With the funding backed by the U.S. government, the lender (in our case, Planters First Bank in Hawkinsville, Georgia) bore little risk in the (hopefully unlikely) event of a default. That type of guarantee was only granted if the SBA knew it could recoup any losses—thus necessitating an ungodly amount of forms, so much so that we retained an SBA specialist to shepherd us through the process. As a lawyer, I was accustomed to the minutiae of legal filings, but the 7(a) loan tested my limits. There were several rounds of submittals, including a narrative explaining why I missed one payment on my Capital One credit card in the past ten years. One payment!

The intense review of my background and finances to qualify for a loan illlustrates how being a later-in-life entrepreneur is an asset. I thankfully had a clean record—no lawsuits, no bankruptcies, no arrests—plus a lifetime of paying bills on time (apart from that one missed payment). That gave me access to capital without having to give up equity. Moreover, age brought an emotional maturity that I lacked in my thirties and even forties. I was learning to accept my vulnerabilities for what they were—my superpowers.

The connections I'd gained through my years in public service were another asset. We got pro bono counseling from the University of Georgia's Small Business Development Center on how to consolidate our two businesses. The SBDC team helped us draft our joint business plan and calculate sales projections needed for the 7(a) loan package. My decades of practicing law were also put to good use. Through networking, we found an excellent firm based in Macon, rather than Atlanta lawyers who charge exorbitant rates, to draft our merger agreement. It's a wealth of experiences that aren't quantified on a balance sheet that are invaluable in starting a business.

In addition to the outside support we enlisted, R.G. read the Harvard Business School's guide to mergers and acquisitions and recommended I do the same. We both reviewed the book so many times that our copies were filled with sticky notes and highlights. It was a great how-to guide on buying a company.

Weeks of preparations and talks culminated in a tour of Atwell Pecans. Seeing the plant in action gave life to the financials we'd been reviewing. The smell of freshly roasted pecans being coated in glaze and chocolate melting in the tempering vats brought flashbacks of touring the Stuckey's candy plant in Eastman with my grandfather. I thought about the hairnetted women who spent their lives lining up perfect rows of fluffy nougat to be packaged as pecan log rolls. The crew at Atwell Pecan decades later were using the same, largely by hand, processes as the Stuckey's ladies did. They were even making the same confections: divinity, pralines, chocolate fudge, and, yes, pecan log rolls. It was uncanny how perfectly aligned this acquisition could be.

The tour concluded with a sit-down meeting. The conference room's mismatched chairs, framed prints of pecan trees, and piles of Folgers Coffee plastic tubs next to the Mr. Coffee maker were a welcome sight. There was no showing off. I was hooked, mess and all. There was only one extravagance: a tray of still-warm pecan confections ushered in by a plant worker. One bite—butter, real vanilla, fresh pecans—was all it took. They were just like my grandmother's recipes made at the Stuckey's candy plant. The feeling that this was right was as strong as the taste.

This was a get-to-know-you meeting with the owner, Jerry Dowdy, who had run Atwell Pecan for decades along with his wife, Susan. Jerry had taken over the plant from his father-in-law and grown operations from shelling to include candy-making. It was a smart move. The candy venture turned what had been an unwanted byproduct—milling loss—into a profitable venture. Milling loss occurs in manufacturing facilities when nuts are cracked and separated from the hull. The pieces are less marketable, as consumers prefer plump halves instead of broken remnants. Adding the candy business, "Orchards Gourmet," introduced Atwell Pecan to a new customer base of specialty shops.

Through the years, Jerry had made other strategic moves, including acquiring a fundraising business, Thames Pecan, that sold chocolate-covered and raw pecans to hundreds of clients across the Southeast, ranging from nonprofits to schools and churches. Jerry was looking to sell it all: the shelling, candy-making, and fundraising businesses. As I learned from the *Harvard Business Review*, ours was an asset purchase as opposed to a stock purchase. We were bidding on the real estate, buildings, and equipment. There were also factors like goodwill, customer accounts, and employee base that were part of the equation.

Jerry had brought his first-in-command to the meeting, a man named Seaborn Dell who had spent his life in the trenches of pecan production. Within a few minutes of asking questions, it was clear that Seaborn was as much a part of the place as the equipment and inventory. He relished knowing how everything worked—there was no production line or piece of machinery that he couldn't fix. While advancing in years, Seaborn was committed to the success of the plant and intended to stay when Jerry retired. His son, Tim, who had been groomed to run the candy operations since working summers there as a teenager, would also remain.

There were layers of complexity to the deal, but the vision of transitioning to manufacturing was simple. It was like a homecoming, bringing us back to the side of the road where my grandfather had his revelation to make candy. This was how Stuckey's had started, and this was how we would restart.

I checked the time and realized I had been inside a concrete building the entire day. I excused myself to stretch my legs and explore the outside of the property. Next door was a gourd farm with a hand-painted sign offering tours. I liked the vibe of having a homey roadside attraction a spitting distance away. I looked across the street. A familiar sight greeted me. In the glow of the end-of-the-day light sat an old Stuckey's store. The telltale features were there: the familiar slope of the roof, remnants of teal paint, latticed grillwork on the front portico. It was now the Dutch House, but all I saw was a Stuckey's.

If there was ever a sign, this was it, like a kindergarten teacher clapping hands for attention. Any second thoughts about moving operations to Wrens and buying this plant were gone when I saw the old Stuckey's. This was what we needed to do.

The following months were consumed with meetings with lawyers, bankers, and intermediaries, hammering out details of the acquisition. We had hoped to close in 2020, but negotiations dragged into the new year. The SBA loan required personal collateral, so R.G. and I pledged everything we owned. It wasn't enough to promise the titles to my home and cars; the bank insisted that I take out a life-insurance policy, with them as the beneficiary. At that point, I was all in. Even my life had become collateral.

It was grueling, but I consider us fortunate. We had a

willing community bank partner that wanted to close the deal. Many promising ventures die from lack of funding. R.G. and I were blessed with solid credit ratings, a lifetime of community connections, and a business that had a rich history with a loyal customer base. All of that weighed in our favor. The demanding process served as a reminder of the advantages I've enjoyed. Despite the sacrifices, it isn't lost on me that my entrepreneurial journey has been made easier by being born with wealth and privilege.

Credit: Eric Ellis

Me & R.G. announcing our business partnership
on September 2, 2020.

We closed on January 31, 2021, in a lawyer's office in Savannah. R.G. and I sat on one side of a long mahogany table in an oak-paneled library lined with law books—a far cry from the cluttered conference room at the candy plant. On the other side sat Jerry and Susan Dowdy. Between us were bankers, lawyers, and documents stacked a foot high. We spent an hour signing our names until my hand ached. I gave up within minutes of any pretense of reading what I was signing, scrawling my name on page after page. When we'd signed the last form, I looked exhaustedly at R.G. "We did it," I said, mustering only a high five and smile. Susan started to cry and wished us all the best. That moment stands out as a reminder that when family businesses change hands, it's as much an emotional process as a financial one. I hugged Susan and assured her we'd do our best to live up to the high standards set by her father and husband. The day was rewarding and draining. All I wanted was a quiet space to let it sink in.

I had rented a farmhouse in Avera for the final week of negotiations. I went back there after the closing and celebrated out in the country with chickens, goats, mules, and even a peacock. I popped a bottle of champagne on the porch, slurping up the bubbles because no one was there to tell me not to. I snapped a selfie on the porch swing. My expression captured what I was feeling—content yet exhausted.

Credit: Stephanie Stuckey

Exhausted but happy. Selfie taken the evening of January 31, 2021, after R.G. and I purchased the Atwell Pecan Plant in Wrens, GA.

In that moment, I felt assured. I took another frothy swig and stared out at the Georgia red clay that stretched for miles, feeling a connectedness that bridged the years between me and my grandfather. Buying a manufacturing plant was a big move, but I was a risk-taker just like him. And also, like him, I was betting on the pecan being the secret to Stuckey's success.

Chapter 6

LIFE IN THE MARGINS

My favorite escape is a used bookstore smelling of old wood and ink, the kind with handwritten staff picks gaily introducing customers to the work of an esoteric author. There's nothing better than opening a well-read book, blotted with the previous owner's coffee stains and scrawled notes in the margins. Words crammed tight with interesting insights or definitions lend much more depth than a new book ordered up on Amazon, hermetically sealed in plastic and pried open with a scrunching sound. I'll take a dog-eared tome still bearing the perfume of its former owner over the impersonality of a new one any day.

That attraction to the margins, to the peripheries of life, is what led me to delve further into a name that curiously appeared on the back of a photograph, smudged in pencil, as I continued to pore over my grandfather's papers in the evenings.

The photo stared out at me from the top of a fresh stack I'd pull to review. Among the images of executives in sporty suits and architectural plans in front of new store sites was one that stood out from the rest. It was my grandfather standing alongside an unfamiliar Black man. Smaller in stature but of sturdy build, the man wore a carefully angled fedora. He gazed uneasily at the camera, perhaps from the sun or shyness.

My grandfather, in contrast, is laughing, as if he and the photographer were in on a private joke. He has one hand confidently in his pocket, like he's about to hand out a big tip, and the other at his side, ready to shake someone's hand. It's a contrast in personas, one looking like he's at the company happy hour, the other unsure he's invited. This photo stood out. The others showing African Americans were all of them inside the plant, pouring caramel, cracking pecans, or packing boxes— not standing outside next to the owner in a fedora hat. There was more to this story. I turned the photo over and read the inscription, "Stuckey with John King at the Candy Plant."

It was getting late. The kids and I were on Sea Island visiting my parents for a long weekend after purchasing the Atwell plant. I'd retreated to Dad's study, the same room where a year and a half ago he'd given me the "lemonade stand" lecture. I'd escaped the nightly after-dinner ritual of watching *The Curse of Oak Island*. From the next room, I could hear my father, full of advice and Jack Daniel's, as he reigned over the family room from his La-Z-Boy throne. His voice, bearing an unmistakable likeness to Foghorn Leghorn, invaded my sanctitude.

"What the hell are you doing?" he bellowed as if the cast were his subjects in the Kingdom of Stuckey. "Don't y'all know the treasure's not there?"

My daughter Beverly's words were inaudible, but I could tell from her pointed tone that she had her own opinions on the subject. I took another sip of the Merlot my parents bought by the case to accommodate the stream of guests that come with owning a beach home. Interrupting this domestic tableau to inquire about John King would cause me to be sucked into the *Oak Island* drama. Like the reality show protagonists, I'd have to discover the truth for myself, unearthing stacks of photos and searching for clues among the old letters and clippings.

After an hour of digging, I found what I was looking for in the special twenty-fifth anniversary edition of *Sweet Talk*, the company newsletter. Unlike the usual monthly editions printed on regular stock paper, this tribute had a glossy silver cover and congratulatory ads from local merchants and vendors. Each was a glowing testimonial to the success of Stuckey's with photos depicting stainless-steel candy machinery, packaging, and other products made for our company. The articles bragged about various store locations, the headquarters at 100 Candy Court, and Stuckey's sales numbers. Dignitaries from local elected officials to the governor sent letters that were reproduced on the pages. And yet the prized spot—the centerfold—was reserved for a photo of my grandfather and John King.

"Who the hell was John King?" I murmured out loud as I finished off the glass a bit too quickly.

The main article relayed the familiar details of our company's founding—the $35 loan from my great-grandmother Cora Lee and the Model A Ford that Bigdaddy drove through the countryside, buying pecans from local farmers. But that wasn't all.

The full story is that he didn't do it alone. John King was with him.

"Stuckey & John," the headline read in a matter-of-fact tone, as if the two were college buddies on a road trip. The reality was far from that. King was a farmhand who worked for my grandfather's family. He was enlisted to drive along in the Model A on those dusty country roads after they'd finished a full day plowing cotton. Exhausted and working late into the evenings, they'd pull over at every house with pecan trees in the yard to buy up that season's crop.

The photo was the same one I'd found earlier, with the two men standing in front of the candy plant, only I noticed more detail this time. King's hand rests uncertainly on the hood of a shiny car, the full length and beauty of it out of his reach. His sleeves are neatly rolled. I imagine he'd been called off his shift for this hastily shot photo. The slanted hat suggests a sense of self and style. My grandfather is beaming beside him, his easy demeanor as bold as the "pecans" sign behind them.

"Back during the Depression," the article read, "when Stuckey first started buying pecans in a 1929 Ford car he took John King, a helper on his father's farm along with him. 'Sometimes business was pretty good and sometimes we didn't do so well, and it looked like them wuz the days we'd get the hungriest.'"

I cringed at how his words had been degraded to a white man's version of how Black men spoke. King's eyes stared out from the page—closing the gap of time—inviting me to look beyond the misspelled words and the grainy image to discover his story. I read on.

"When we'd talk about eatin' dinner on them days . . ." More cringeworthiness.

"Mr. Stuckey'd say, 'John, you just get back there and eat some more pecans.'" This line was intended to be humorous, a witty story told at the company retreat over cigars and martinis.

"True or not," the article went on, "they both remember the hard times they had, and John has been eating pecans ever since. He takes on other odd jobs at times, but always comes back to Stuckey's, which is home."

I took off my reading glasses, a concession to age I'd accepted in my fifties, and rubbed the corners of my eyes. It was hard to read: The man who'd been reduced to a pecan diet in those early days, while helping my grandfather become fabulously successful, had led a rambling life of odd jobs. Yet Stuckey's was home. Or was it?

The article cheerfully concluded with, "John and Stuckey probably are about the same age. Both are very healthy looking and the 'pecan diet' has proven highly successful for each of them."

I let out an audible "hmmmmph!" just as my father poked his head in the door.

"Why are you reading through all that old stuff? Quit rummaging through Bigdaddy's papers and go make some money!" My father often opted for commands over advice. I waved my empty wineglass at him in a dismissive gesture and rummaged through the box like I'd dropped an earring.

Shaking his head and muttering, "You're going to bankrupt the business," he started to shut the door when I interrupted him.

"Who was John King?"

"Who was who?" he asked, cocking his head as if to blame his hearing aids for the lapse.

"John King," I said, louder than intended.

"Good God, you don't have to shout! I'm not deaf yet." But he stopped in the doorway and gazed over my head as if capturing a memory. "Strongest man I ever met. John King could lift fifty-five bags of pecans all day long." He paused. "Why?"

"Curious why he was featured in the twenty-fifth anniversary edition of *Sweet Talk*," I said, holding up the picture.

"Well, he was just always around, from the beginning. Worked all sorts of jobs. A good man."

"Do you know how I could track down his family?"

"Good God! Seriously, pull your head out of those papers and focus on making money."

I stared at him pleadingly like I was a child again and he'd taken me to the toy store.

"I'm sure some of Boots's kinfolk would know. Call the Fluellens." With that, he ended the conversation with a click of the door, his footsteps trailing as he cut out lights and headed to bed.

I slid open the French doors that led to the pool and hot tub with a starlit view of the marsh. I sunk in one of the lounge chairs and thought about that name I hadn't heard in a stretch of time.

Boots Fluellen.

He'd been my grandfather's driver, a slender Black man who was always immaculately dressed with polished shoes and a dapper chauffeur's cap. They'd travel the dusty back roads from Eastman to St. Simons for weekend jaunts, my grandfather sporting Hawaiian shirts and khaki pants while Boots would be elegantly attired in his full-on uniform just in case a change of plans required a detour to the Waldorf Astoria. Bigdaddy and Boots were practically inseparable; folks would rarely see one without the other. Yet, there was a separateness about them in the racially segregated South.

One story told to me by my aunt Lynda, my father's younger sister and my grandparents' only other child, painfully illustrates this. Bigdaddy and Boots were driving from Eastman to the Georgia coast. They were taking separate cars, as my grandfather had a friend with him. Boots was charged with driving the friend's car. My grandfather had a lead foot and raced ahead. Boots, by contrast, kept to the speed limit, mindful that if you were Black in the South you obeyed the law or risked untold brutalities at the hands of small-town sheriffs. Despite his precautions, a blue light soon flashed in Boots's rearview mirror. Without my grandfather as his protector, Boots had no choice but to press on the gas. He engaged in a high-speed chase for several minutes until he thankfully caught up with my grandfather. Cutting in front of Bigdaddy's car, Boots motioned frantically for him to pull over. The irate patrolman stormed out of the car, his gun drawn and at the ready, only to discover Mr. Stuckey, who was well known at that point, parked in between them, demanding to know what the hell was going on. A tragedy was thankfully averted, but this incident shows the racial realities of that era.

When Bigdaddy died, Boots moved to working for my grandmother. It was an awkward transition; the headstrong matriarch didn't need looking after. Every year, she'd buy the latest Cadillac, trading in the old model as easily as she'd change shoes. Chain-smoking menthol cigarettes with the air-conditioning cranked on high, she cruised around Dodge County, her charm bracelet dangling against the steering wheel whenever she hit a hard turn. A driver, even one as trusted as Boots in his nappy uniform, would cramp her Southern queen bee style. Family members intervened. With Bigdaddy gone, she needed a watchful eye. What if her car broke down or ran out of gas on some desolate back road? The latter scenario was as remote as the scavengers on *The Curse of Oak Island* hitting gold. My grandmother always drove with a full tank of gas. But the point had been made. Boots was kept in the family employ and a compromise reached as to his new duties. He was to be my grandmother's companion, at the ready if any slight misfortune befell her. But Bigmama insisted on doing her own driving.

And so a curious sight became commonplace on the streets of Eastman: my grandmother driving her sleek new-model Cadillac with Boots, in his pressed chauffeur's uniform, dutifully sitting in the back seat. A bizarre reverse version of *Driving Miss Daisy*.

At one point, most of the Fluellen family worked for Stuckey's. The story I recall best is about Boots's brother, who everyone called Bymonitious. It was an unusual name with a troubling origin. One day, while he was in Congress, Dad was helping Bymonitious apply for his Social Security benefits, which required listing one's full name. "I'm embarrassed, Bymonitious, that I've known you my whole life, but I don't know your real name," Dad admitted sheepishly.

"Robert James Fluellen," the elderly man replied politely.

"Well, how on earth did you get a name like Bymonitious?" Dad exclaimed.

"Well, sir, back when your father hired me, he asked me, 'What do they call you?' And I said, 'By my initials,' because as a boy everyone called me 'R.J.'" My grandfather, who was hard of hearing, mistook that to be his name.

And the name stuck. Because in the 1940s in the rural South, a young Black man didn't talk back to a white man, even to correct an honest mistake. He endured a lifetime of carrying a name that wasn't his, his identity disguised by misunderstanding and racism.

That the Fluellen family might be a link to King made sense. I remember driving to their various family homes on the other side of the tracks throughout my childhood. Back then, the railroad line dividing Eastman was as impenetrable as the Berlin Wall. The white families lived north of the tracks in their porticoed homes and manicured lawns while the south side was reserved for the Black families who raised the white children, cooked their meals, cleaned their homes, and—as I was to learn in a very real and personal way—built their businesses.

As a child growing up in Washington, D.C., in classrooms with Black kids whose parents were diplomats, elected officials, high-powered lobbyists, and Pentagon generals, the world I ventured into every summer to spend time with family was as foreign as another country.

"Our Blacks aren't like your Blacks," one of my great-aunts who worked as a substitute teacher in Dodge County would explain to me in a hushed, knowing tone. "It's different here."

That same aunt would warn me "not to go wandering over to n---- town," as if south of the tracks were infested with crime and ill-repute. How could the warmhearted Willie Mae who helped raise me—as generous with hugs as she was with switches—or the fast-talking, gum-smacking Vera, who whipped up turnip greens, fried corn, butter beans, and sixteen-layer caramel cake in my grandmother's kitchen, live in a place my aunt dismissed as "nothing but trouble"?

Despite the occasional protest, like going to the movies

in downtown Eastman on "n--- night"—an unspoken truce reached between Blacks and whites of the town that Wednesday nights would be reserved for the Blacks—I'd accepted as a child that things were different where I came from. There were moments of genuine kindness that bridged the gap that split our town. But the pervasive air of separateness lingered as thick as the humidity.

Back in my father's study, I checked my phone. It was 2 AM, and the late hour was wearing on me. I headed for bed, determined to start tracking down the Fluellens and John King in the morning.

———

Days turned into weeks, chasing dead-end leads about John King. I reread the biography of my grandfather published by Macon University and found an account of how King and my grandfather had worked so hard and so late in those early days that they often slept on top of the pecan bags between stretches of farmhouses. John King, the interview continued, would later work for Stuckey's and eventually own his own Stuckey's store. The idea that an African American during the Jim Crow Era was "gifted" a store in his name was practically unheard of in the Deep South and fueled my resolve to learn more.

The Fluellens turned out to be as much a fool's errand as the search for gold on *Oak Island*. While there were recollections of King, no details or leads to his family emerged. But the Fluellen clan led me to another prospect, an old family friend, Dwight Goolsby, who'd grown up with some of the King sons. John King, it turns out, had been prolific later in life. He married a woman much his junior and had eight children by her. He died in his sixties, leaving his young widow with a large family to raise alone.

One of the benefits of a small town is that kindness is often remembered for generations. The Stuckeys and the Goolsbys have been exchanging small favors for decades, which built deposits of goodwill. Race relations in the South are messy and complicated. Despite the gaps in wealth and opportunity, families like the Goolsbys and the Stuckeys— one Black and one white—are forever bound by place and history. Dwight could call me in the middle of the night in need of help, and I'd do whatever he needed, no questions asked.

As expected, when I reached out to him after a few years' absence, Dwight didn't hesitate to switch into action. Like any true Southerner, Dwight could recite from memory— handed down from generations of front-porch talking—the lineage of families in our small town and how we were all connected.

"There was a whole bunch of them Kings," he joked with a whistle to make his point. As efficient as a spelling bee contestant, Dwight pronounced the names of King family members, detailing how they had intersected with the various clans in Eastman. He recalled that one of John King's sons was named Sylvester (after Bigdaddy himself), but he'd have to ask around about the others. I found myself slipping into the easy colloquialism of my roots.

"Yes, I reckoned as much. Like the Fluellens, you could shake a stick and find a few dozen."

"You got that right, sugar." Dwight laughed. "Give me a few days, I'll track the King sons down for you," he said conspiratorially, as if tasked with a secret mission.

As had become the custom when I called folks from home, I finished the call promising to send a case of pecan log rolls. This was never requested, but it was an unspoken expectation created by my grandfather and perpetuated by my father. Folks in Dodge County were used to us Stuckeys—whether we owned the company or not—having an endless supply of the sugary sweetness that defined our family.

I hung up the phone, encouraged that one of the King children had been named Sylvester. John and my grandfather must have been close. Why else would he name one of his sons after him?

Or maybe not. I grimaced, recalling a story I'd heard as a child that I'd dismissed as a trumped-up tale, a cross-town telephone game that grew more exaggerated over the years. It involved Big Herman, a burly Black man who ran a lawn service catering to the best families in Eastman. The bridge club ladies circuit vied for Big Herman to tend to their gardenias and crepe myrtles, a fierce competition to get the "yard of the month" sign planted in their yard.

The story went that Big Herman named one of his sons "Sylvester" after my grandfather. Flattered by this unexpected gesture, Bigdaddy gifted the newborn with a $100 U.S. savings bond. Within a few weeks, another Black child was named Sylvester, and my grandfather gave another bond to that newborn. However, within a few months, almost all the baby boys on the south side of town were named "Sylvester," leaving my grandfather to rethink his generosity. The naming bonus was discontinued, and the glut of Sylvesters in Eastman came to a close. I've always wondered how the beleaguered schoolteachers managed a classroom full of Sylvesters during those years.

Was Sylvester King a product of this brief window in time, the choice of name motivated by money, not affection? Or was the story just the stuff of rural legend? Some truths are better left unknown, I concluded. Especially in a place like Eastman where revelations can unearth a small-town Pandora's box.

———

True to his word, Dwight followed up a week later with phone numbers for Horace and Sylvester, two of the eight King children. Days of messaging back and forth finally yielded brief conversations with the sons. While they were both helpful and willing to share what details they remembered, it wasn't the big reveal I'd been seeking. The men had been very young when their later-in-life father had passed away, their memories almost as faded as the photos I had of him. Yet, like furniture that needed rearranging in a cluttered room, the story was slowly forming a narrative with each new piece of information.

I learned from his sons that John King had worked for

Stuckey's most of his life, with a variety of jobs including making signs at the shop next to the day care the King children attended. One son recalled his father coming out between breaks to speak to them through the chain-link fence that separated the shop from the playground.

My grandfather used to pick their dad up for fishing weekends in Florida, leaving Friday after work and not returning until late Sunday. Whether King was working on these weekends or brought along as part of the fishing trip is unclear; the truth may have been a mix of both. Another recollection was their mother being picked up by a chauffeur sent by my grandfather every Christmas to attend the Stuckey's holiday party for years after their father had died.

As for a Stuckey's store, whether one was promised or not is unclear. But what is known is that John King never owned a Stuckey's. I was disappointed to learn this, hoping that he was rewarded for being part of those early, hard years hauling pecans, plus remaining part of the company for the bulk of his life.

While the full story remains lost to time, this is what I believe to be true: John King was much more than the details I learned. He represents generations of Black men in this country, particularly in the South, who helped build white wealth without any credit. Men whose lives are memorialized in photos in company archives, buried in boxes crammed under beds. Much more fascinating to me than unearthing gold is discovering the stories of these people who contributed so much, yet the truth of their lives may never be known.

There were other John Kings at Stuckey's—the hundreds of African Americans who toiled long hours in our candy plant, stirring copper cauldrons of egg whites and sugar to boiling temperatures and lifting pallets of product from the loading docks day in and day out. They drove our trucks, grilled burgers at our snack bar, and painted our signs.

Credit: Stuckey's Archives

Bigdaddy and John King: This photo was featured in the centerfold of the 25th anniversary edition of the Stuckey's company newsletter.

Men like Fred McDowell, a Mississippi singer best known for his hit song, "You Got to Move," which was covered by the Rolling Stones on their *Sticky Fingers* album. In the late 1960s and early 1970s, his day job was pumping gas at the Stuckey's off I-55 at Exit 310 in Como. As McDowell didn't own a phone, the store served as an improbable office for the legendary bluesman, where he fielded calls from clubs and New York agents in between servicing cars. The other employees got used to hearing people with strange accents on the other end of the line: "We've got Paris, France, on the phone, Fred." Even after he was in high demand at international clubs and festivals and able to support himself with his music, McDowell returned to Stuckey's and Como when he wasn't touring, according to the book *Blues Traveling* by Steve Cheseborough. McDowell worked for Stuckey's for years, a stark contrast to his musical career.

Credit: Stuckey's Archives

Boots Fluellen (in chauffer's cap) with other
unidentified employees of Stuckey's.

I struggled with whether to reveal this part of our story to a contemporary audience in the era of Black Lives Matter, potentially subjecting my family to criticism and rebuke.

But I can't tell our story without telling the stories of John King, the Fluellen family, Fred McDowell, and countless others whose names are lost to time. The details of their lives, except for McDowell, may be scant, but they deserve more than a brief mention in the margins. They deserve a chapter. My words are insufficient to convey the depth of my emotions about their lives and contributions to our prosperity. If King, Boots and R.J. Fluellen, and McDowell had been white, would they have risen to be vice presidents, owned stores, and been financially well off? Probably so. I can't rewrite history or change the past, but I can honor it and the lives that have made a difference.

Thank you to all the men and women who helped build Stuckey's and have never been recognized. I am forever grateful.

Chapter 7

LESSONS LEARNED
ON THE FRONT LINES
OF CANDYLAND

S mall-town diners make you feel like you belong;
plates piled high with comfort food like macaroni and
cheese, chicken fried steak, and black-eyed peas wel-
coming even "foreigners" from exotic places like New York
City. The placemats double as menus, and the walls are lined
with photos of the local little league team. While it may lack
a movie theater, brew pub, or Walmart, Wrens, Georgia,
population 2,180—like so many towns across America—
boasts a charming "meat and three" that is the heartbeat of
the community.

With coffee strong enough to slap you awake freshly
brewing at 6 AM, Peggy's is where you'll find everyone from

the county sheriff to the Dollar General cashiers mingling before their shifts. One morning, a few months after acquiring Atwell Pecan Company, a fixture on Main Street since 1935, I stopped by Peggy's for breakfast. It was 7 AM, and I was among the latecomers, the regulars already on their third cups. I had on blue jeans, boots caked in caramel glaze, and a Stuckey's cap, ready for a day of meetings interspersed with walks on the candy plant floor. The old-timers at the front table were griping about the price of cotton and commenting on every truck that drove by. They looked me over, bemused by the novelty of a stranger. "Hey, pretty lady," one of them said, a remark that would have irked me a decade earlier but, at age fifty-five, I accepted gratefully. "Hey there," I shot back in my best Southern twang, trying to fit in. He eyed the logo on my ball cap. "I bet you work at the Stuckey's plant down the road," mispronouncing it as "Stew-key." Instead of correcting him, I just smiled. "I sure do," I answered proudly. His overall-clad companion glanced up from *The News and Farmer* and drily noted, "Betcha get to eat all them pecan log rolls you want for free!" I winked at them, "It's the best part of the job." The whole restaurant laughed. I realized there are no private conversations at Peggy's. The waitress walked over with a cup of coffee that I had not ordered. "Welcome," she said. "We're glad you're here." While I had not been inducted into the local Rotary or Kiwanis Club, getting that cup of diner coffee was just as gratifying as being handed a membership pin.

That moment reinforced how we were doing something more than simply buying a company. R.G. and I were becoming part of a community. The *Harvard Business Review*, as thorough as it was, needed a second volume titled "And Now What?" As soon as the paperwork is executed and the ink is dry, the transaction itself is done. Yet there is a whole other aspect to acquiring a plant that involves culture and community. The dealmaking is the easier part. Earning trust and forging relationships over a lifetime is the hard part that really matters.

This was something I learned from my grandfather, mining his archives for nuggets on how to build community while building a business. It's different when you acquire a company like R.G. and I had done. We had to respect the history of what came before. I spent time researching the background of the Atwell Pecan Company and learned that our two businesses and families had a rich history and friendship.

———

Royce Atwell founded his company in 1935; the same time my grandfather first started selling pecans in Eastman, a two-hour drive southwest of Wrens. Both companies flourished during the postwar economic boom, and my grandfather even sourced pecans for Stuckey's log rolls from Mr. Atwell. When Stuckey's added a sign painting company to accommodate the growing need for billboards on the highways, we made the sign at the Atwell Pecan Company. Not to mention, of course, the Stuckey's store just across the road, which was built in the 1960s. My aunt Jane and uncle J.H.

owned that store at one point, and my cousins, Lynn and Tim, lived there.

Royce Atwell, like my grandfather, sold his business after growing it into a profitable venture. He fortunately fared better than Bigdaddy with his choice of successors in Hugh Oliver, who brought in his son-in-law, Jerry Dowdy, to manage the business. Although Jerry's wife, Susan, had grown up around the pecan shelling business, Jerry, a recent graduate of the University of Georgia and only twenty-three years old, had no experience in the field.

Oliver espoused a business philosophy similar to my grandfather's: hire good people with common sense and train them. Jerry moved to Wrens and learned by doing, managing the operations while Susan worked in the office.

Over the span of several decades, the Dowdys modernized the facility and expanded operations. As luck would have it, their lineup of confections included a pecan log roll that was as good as the ones Stuckey's made when I was a child.

These commonalities matter, as does a shared belief in hard work and an attachment to family and place. It's the intangible factors that are often overlooked in acquisition deals. But, after the handshaking was over, this is what enabled us to merge our companies in real life as well as on paper.

While the ownership had changed, we were intent on keeping the leadership intact. R.G. had done the due diligence of meeting individually with the plant managers and gotten commitments that they would stay on board after the transition to Stuckey's. Seaborn and his son, Tim, who we promoted to head of the candy operations, were instrumental in keeping the machines running, the clients happy, and the workforce stable.

———————

It takes hands-on management to run a manufacturing facility. You must physically be present to drive productivity. This was the most challenging aspect of being CEO, as I remained in Atlanta. While my son had left for college at Auburn University, my daughter, Beverly, was still in Atlanta. She was a freshman in high school, having recently survived the angst-ridden middle school years and emerged with a trusted friend group and a learning environment where she thrived. I needed to remain in Atlanta until Beverly graduated. Four years of commuting several times a week was an easy sacrifice compared to the struggles of moving a fourteen-year-old used to city living to a rural town with a population of less than three thousand.

Fortunately, R.G. was willing to move with his family— his wife, Rachel, who was pregnant with their second child, and his young daughter, Lizzie—to Augusta. We agreed that R.G. would be the lead in running the pecan operations along with Seaborn while I worked remotely, in charge of marketing and sales. I am forever grateful for a business partnership that recognizes that family comes first.

Valuing family extends beyond your relatives. My grandfather taught me that creating a company culture where all

are respected like members of a family is what drove his success. That sense of specialness and belonging extends to everyone who interacts with your business, from the employees
to the vendors and customers. My grandfather would rise at
dawn to greet the candy plant shift workers by name as they
arrived and drive for hours to visit the Stuckey's stores in
person. While business meetings and desk work are important, that consistent presence with your team is what builds
morale and motivation, just like how steadily being there for
your children is what strengthens your relationships.

Every week, I get messages from former employees of
Stuckey's, excited to learn that we're making a comeback.
Most of these folks haven't worked for us in decades, yet
they recount their experiences with our company as if they
just occurred. I treasure these communications and refer to
them frequently; they're more motivational than any self-
help book. This sticking power is almost unimaginable in
today's world where few employees spend their entire careers
with the same company. As we reinvent Stuckey's in modern
times, we aim to keep some things exactly the same. That
sense of family within our team and out in the community
is something that I hope remains unchanged and lives on
today.

———

Who you hire reflects your priorities. The first new hire we
made at the candy plant was a human resources director. It
was February of 2021. People were still coming down with

COVID-19, and we were dealing with frequent worker short-ages. Moreover, Amazon announced the construction of a new distribution facility only twenty-eight miles down the road, promising higher wages. Knowing employees' names is one thing, but without the foundation of a healthy, well-paid workforce, none of our efforts to create a workplace culture could succeed.

We turned to one of the best resources for small businesses: a seasoned professional nearing retirement. Mike Hawn had spent his career in operations and human resources in the food business. Ready to slow down, he wanted to put his experience to use with a few select consulting gigs. Mike was a welcome addition to our growing team. We initially hired him on a contract basis to draft a pay scale that would reward the longer-term employees and incentivize new recruits, along with a training program to allow increases for completion of new skills and certifications. We soon found him invaluable, bringing him on as a salaried employee. Mike has grown to be as passionate about reviving Stuckey's as we are.

Mike helped us navigate the morass of health care programs and put in place benefits that were both comprehensive and within our budget. It's ironic how life comes full circle, as my years in the Georgia legislature as a Democrat often pitted me on the labor side of employment debates. I advocated for companies to provide more comprehensive health care plans without an appreciation of the sometimes-crippling impact on small businesses. I met with constituents who shared their struggles with chronic conditions like diabetes, unable to gain access to affordable treatments. The CEOs of large corporations testifying about how we needed to be mindful of controlling costs rang hollow with me as an idealistic legislator.

Now, some thirty years later, I'm grappling with these issues as I sit in the CEO's seat, albeit of a small company struggling to make a comeback. Health care for our candy plant in a rural community with a head count of almost a hundred costs Stuckey's hundreds of thousands of dollars a year. This is a significant line item on our budget. While the pendulum hasn't swung to the other extreme in my views, my life experiences have informed a more empathetic approach to the demands of running a business. Those 3 AM moments of waking up anxious about meeting payroll are real, as are my recollections of my former constituents who couldn't afford medications or critical care.

Our shelling and candy operations in Wrens and the distribution center in Eastman were slowly coming together as one. It was tough work to integrate financials, payroll, software systems, and human resources. We held a retreat with the leadership team and drafted a strategic plan. Weekly executive team meetings were held to check progress on production, sales, and financial goals. Gradually, we started to see modest gains in progress and revenue.

It was during one of these Monday morning calls that a mundane review of our accounts payable led to a critical shift in how we did business. We were going through our list of outstanding debts, many of them delinquent for over a year to vendors that supplied us with the tchotchkes sold in Stuckey's stores. Our bills had stacked up to the point where we were on restricted payment terms with many of our vendors.

In order to get back in good graces, we had created the "Thousand Dollar Club," whereby we would pay our creditors $1,000/month until our balances were paid in full. During the weekly A/P review, we arrived at one account that was significantly in arrears, with the explanation that the vendor hadn't requested payment. After years of surviving with limited cash flow, Stuckey's had eased into a routine of nonpayment. "Maybe we just let that one slide for now," I commented. R.G. interjected, "That's not how we do business. If we owe them money, we pay them. Invoice or no invoice—they belong in the Thousand Dollar Club with the others."

It was a financial stretch for us to resolve these debts. Yet character reveals itself in moments when it's hard to do the right thing. The days of Stuckey's dodging our debts like a prizefighter dancing around the ring were over. The culture of the company was returning to its roots of treating everyone like a friend. That meant making good on our obligations.

It was a seemingly minor moment but one that helped define our culture. Being trustworthy has a ripple effect. A year later, I was working a trade show when I visited the booth of the vendor that R.G. insisted we add to the Thousand Dollar Club. The vendor immediately recognized me and thanked me for paying off our debt. He had just gotten a shipment of bead necklaces and gave us a great deal on them. He saw me eyeing a bucket hat with bright yellow bananas. "It's yours," he said. "As a thank-you for how you've treated us." It's now one of my favorite possessions, totally silly and fun. I take it with me on road trips as a reminder that doing the right thing can lead to a sense of community, trusted relationships . . . and even a ridiculous banana hat.

Credit: Stephanie Stuckey

My Favorite Hat: The banana bucket hat is a reminder
to always treat people right and do the right thing.

One of the most trying aspects of merging corporate entities was the design and packaging. We decided to maintain
the snack brand that RG had founded, Front Porch Pecans.
He had cultivated a niche market within the health food and
Keto diet sectors that generated consistent sales. The other
products that bore the Stuckey's name had been outsourced
to third-party manufacturers or co-packers for decades. We
had several different food facilities that were private labeling
our snack nuts, pecan log rolls, pralines, chocolate turtles,
and divinity.

Conversely, the Orchards Gourmet also had third-party
manufacturing deals for retail clients, mostly ones that offered "fresh from the farm"–type fare. They produced a full
line of specialty candies and seasoned nuts, including pecans,
almonds, and cashews. The labels were designed in-house
and packaged by the team in Wrens. With us managing both
sides of these deals, my impromptu education in running a
business had quickly added a crash course in Co-Packing 101.

I naively thought that transitioning to us making Stuckey's products again would be an expedient matter of giving
notice to our co-packers and then starting manufacturing
in-house. But these outsourcing arrangements included
packaging that was paid for by the third-party vendors
and baked into our overall costs. For us to terminate contracts early would mean those packaging costs—often tens
of thousands of dollars—would be eaten by us. While large
companies like Hershey's and M&M Mars routinely change

designs and can afford to absorb those costs, smaller outfits like Stuckey's would have to wait until our packaging stock was depleted. Unfortunately, this resulted in our new product and packaging rolling out in stages based on when we could transition to manufacturing in-house, SKU by SKU. In a few cases, we would lose a couple of thousand dollars to streamline the progression more smoothly. But, overall, this was another setback that honed my patience skills.

There are two aspects to these outsourcing arrangements—the external design of the package and the internal quality of the product. Both are equally essential. Over the years of having our Stuckey's snacks and candies outsourced, we lost much of what made our brand special and unique. The yellow outline in our logo was altered to a fluorescent hue, reminiscent of an '80s Spencer's mall store vibe. The photograph on the cover of our Hunkey Dorey was an unappetizing pile of coagulated popcorn and caramel. And the most egregious example was one package that mistakenly listed our founding year as 1924, an error that could have been corrected by a five second Google search.

The product itself was also lacking. We had operated in survival mode for so long that cutting corners on ingredients had become routine. Nothing was more critical than sourcing only the highest-quality fresh-crop pecans. My grandfather had prided himself on his ability to select the best pecans, dating back to his early years when he memorized the different varieties by labeling paper bags. With the acquisition of a company that had been in the pecan business since 1935, we were returning to our agrarian roots. As quickly as we could run through the packaging with our outsourcing partners, Stuckey's would return—after a fifty-year hiatus—to once again using only Georgia fresh-crop pecans.

As we waited out the various co-packing arrangements, R.G. and I busied ourselves with the new design work, our logo being the most crucial. With a nostalgic brand, there is a wealth of material to build upon. I studied my grandfather's archives for images of our old packaging, billboards, early promotions, and copy. I loved the elegant and snazzy phrasing of this *Mad Men* era of advertising. The stylishly attired women in dresses and men in hats on their Sunday drives, pulling over at Stuckey's for our "Hurry-Up Snacks," "Picturesque Souvenirs," and "Sparkling Rest Rooms." One pamphlet promised that "any trip's a pleasure trip when you stop at Stuckey's." Travelers who were "pleasure bound" could find our "tasty treats" on "main highways most everywhere." We wanted to capture the sophistication and class of a road trip in that bygone era with a contemporary freshness.

I interviewed several boutique firms. They submitted impressive proposals for our redesign, with equally impressive budgets that were beyond our means. Fearing I'd have to resort to a cut-rate freelancer on Fiverr, I turned to Instagram for inspiration. Scrolling through the search results for #vintagedesign, I discovered an artist named Mack Fraga whose aesthetic matched that of Stuckey's. His posts were filled with old-school signage, toys, and whimsey, with attention to font and typeset. Mack had examples of packaging he'd done for a retro toy line that included X-ray vision glasses, kazoos, and fortune-telling cards. It was nostalgic with an edgy hipness to it.

I messaged Mack that I loved his work. Within an hour, I received a response that he remembered Stuckey's and stopped there as a kid. "We should talk," I messaged back and included my number. My phone rang almost immediately. I was visiting my parents at the time, sitting on their deck overlooking the marsh on the Georgia coast. The sun was starting to set when Mack called, and it was full-on darkness by the time our conversation ended.

Mack had plenty of work and wasn't looking to take on clients but had a soft spot for our brand. Moreover, he saw the opportunity that relaunching a classic brand like ours held for someone with his talents and vision. We negotiated a contract within our budget and added a second designer, Dave Bahm, who worked with Mack and supplemented his design work. The two of them made a dynamic design duo that was critical to our new branding.

Our first chance to roll out new packaging was with our 2.5-ounce classic confection line. Our cello wrap supply was depleted at the company that had been making our pralines, turtles, and divinity. We were anxious to not have a gap in production and carefully timed the transition to manufacturing in-house. The new rolls of film with Mack's beautiful design arrived just in time to fill orders for our stores and accounts. We did several test runs and sampled the candies. Everything tasted and looked perfect. Unfortunately, we were about to experience our first major setback.

When bad stuff happens, it often sneaks up like a few

clouds in the sky that quickly turn into pummeling rain. It started with a negative review. I personally monitor the online comments posted about Stuckey's on Yelp, Google, social media sites like Facebook and LinkedIn, and www.stuckeys.com, where customers can write in our guestbook. I take this feedback seriously, figuring that for every negative review there were a dozen others with the same experience who didn't take the time to complain and simply decided not to buy our product again.

"I bought the divinity at a Stuckey's in Perry, Georgia," wrote Hal G. "It smelled and tasted like glue. Yuck!" I took a screenshot and sent it to Vicki Cannington, one of the few legacy Stuckey's employees. Vicki managed customer service and knew our company history and products inside and out. I also texted our senior sale representative, Jim Schelble, another long-term employee. I asked them both to be on the lookout for similar complaints and considered the matter resolved.

Within a few days, however, another complaint emerged. This one from someone at the candy plant who also detected an unpleasant odor and taste in the pralines. By week's end, there were a handful of complaints from different sources all related to products that had been packaged in the new cello film.

I drove two and a half hours to our warehouse in Eastman to personally check on the batches. The odor was faint, and I found the taste to be unaffected. We got mixed feedback from the various tests we conducted among our employees, most agreeing there was a glue-like smell but differing on whether the flavor was impacted. R.G. and Tim also ran tests in Wrens, with similar results.

We faced an existential crisis of whether to continue shipping out questionable product or hold all orders and pull the product that had already shipped. We had orders that were due and would incur penalties for late delivery. Plus, we would owe credits to all the stores that would have the product pulled. We made the wrong choice and gave the go-ahead to continue filling orders with the new film. By the end of week two, the problem persisted with more complaints. Given that we had thousands of boxes on shelves across the Southeast, it was still minor in comparison. But it was enough of a threat to our reputation that we were taking serious notice.

R.G. and I schooled ourselves on food safety laws and learned the distinction between a voluntary product withdrawal, which occurs when there is a quality issue but no health risk, and an involuntary product recall, when federal law mandates product removal as a threat to human health. Our investigation revealed that the offensive odor was caused by the adhesive our packaging company had used to seal layers of plastic together. The issue was exacerbated by the thick coating, which didn't allow gases to escape. Moreover, pralines and divinity are particularly absorbent to flavors and seasonings, ideal for candy-making but less so if offensive odors are sealed in an airtight package.

The good news was that we were not legally obligated to withdraw the product, nor, thankfully, was there any risk to the safety and well-being of our customers. But on the flip side was the negative impact on our brand. After much discussion and internal soul searching, R.G. and I made the hard but right decision to withdraw the product.

We were on the cusp of Q4 sales, the busiest and most profitable time of the year, yet were facing a shortfall in inventory, a decline in sales, and issuing credits for hundreds of stores that had been sent cases of faulty product. While our packaging company gave us a credit toward future orders to make amends, we took a financial hit at a time when we could least afford to do so. As tempting as it was to brush the issue aside and continue filling orders for pralines and divinity bars, we bit the proverbial bullet and did the right thing by our clients and our company's reputation.

It's vital to debrief after setbacks. It's the challenges, not the successes, that offer the best guidance in business and in life. The packaging tsunami taught us a lot about food safety laws. It also taught us to act decisively, as delay is rarely your ally when problems arise. And, most importantly, I learned that doing the right thing is always the right thing, despite how hard it is in the moment of crisis.

Chapter 8

THE ROADSIDE STAND GROWS UP

Selling pecans was at the core of everything my grandfather did. From the time he learned how to distinguish one variety of nut from the other, he knew that Georgia's abundant resource was his ticket to prosperity.

By the late 1930s, his modest roadside stand offering my grandmother's homemade candies had matured into a real enterprise. He made enough to invest in a warehouse in downtown Eastman. Soon, the entrance was crowded with large bins filled with Stuarts, Pawnees, Elliots, and Papershells. He would sell anywhere from a few pounds to a bushel—anything to make a buck. The country was emerging from the Great Depression, and Bigdaddy joined thousands of other small businesses in America as part of the economic rebound.

Sales were solid, and he was soon showing enough of a profit to qualify for a loan from the Bank of Eastman for $600. This was a sizeable bump from his grandmother's $35. It was enough for Bigdaddy to buy more inventory and a pickup truck, a welcome upgrade from the Model A that was ill-suited for hauling pecans on gravelly dirt roads. He had learned to value pecans for himself without enlisting a buyer, saving costs and, most importantly, becoming independent and self-assured in his abilities. This college dropout had created his own de facto MBA, trading the classroom for pecan groves; his curriculum being the study of the shape, size, and color of nuts; his profit the final grade. These experiences didn't translate into a bullet item on a resume, but they transformed him from a blue jean–clad product of the Depression to a savvy entrepreneur in pressed pants and linen shirts.

Every business claims a notch on a timeline that is its start date. It becomes a fixture on their logo, a mark of continuity and stability. For Stuckey's, that year was 1937. That was when my grandfather got another, larger loan from a big city bank in Macon, Georgia. He transitioned from his warehouse to the first brick-and-mortar Stuckey's along Route 23 in Eastman.

Bigdaddy aimed to build "The South's Most Famous Candy Shoppe," as the sign out front bragged. He wanted something that would catch the eye, enough to entice hurried motorists to press on their brakes or make a U-turn.

Three shiny glass-topped pumps, bright red and olive green, stood sentry out front, offering gas for a few cents a gallon. He fashioned a logo from his own signature. The bold curve of the *S* was bookended with a thick top and bottom, followed by a *T* with a cross that extended over the *U* and the *C* like a trumpet blaring, "I'm heeeeeere!" The letters rushed to the apostrophe and a sassy *S* with a curved tail. The logo was painted in red and yellow on the roof—as loud as the bravado of the owner of this roadside curiosity.

Credit: Stuckey's Archives

Where It All Began: The first Stuckey's store in Eastman, GA.
A later version of the building with the classic sloped blue roof
is still there today, though sadly abandoned and in disrepair.

There were no apps to signal his store was just up the road. To tempt travelers away from their map-drawn routes, Bigdaddy painted a dripping orange on the side of the building along with "Ice Cold Juice" and "Farm Fresh Hams."

111

Three Coca-Cola signs topped the gas canopy like points on a crown. A snack bar offered on-the-go meals of grilled cheese and hot dogs. The store also sold quilts, Kewpie dolls, coloring books, souvenir plates, and nickel trinkets geared toward wives and restless back-seat children. An astute observer of human nature, Bigdaddy studied what customers wanted and created a fun diversion from the tedium of driving.

He'd invested heavily on this concept, and the gamble paid off. The store grossed $30,000 that first year, enough to open a second store in 1939. The next location off Highway 41 in Unadilla was along the Florida tourist route, welcoming road-weary families with clean restrooms, ice water, a tankful of gas, and—of course—tasty pecan treats.

The stores were successful, but the Depression mindset never left him. During this time and throughout his life, Bigdaddy continued to have "just in case" backups like several Black juke joints, selling railroad crossties, a car dealership, and a funeral home. These side hustles proved successful in their own right but also helped finance his growing Stuckey's operations.

Bigdaddy added another Stuckey's in Folkston, Georgia, in 1941. Along the Florida state line on U.S. 1, he joked that he was following migratory northern tourists as they flocked like birds to warmer destinations.

The candy for these early stores was made on-site according to Ethel and the bridge club's original recipes: pralines, fudge, divinity, and pecan log rolls. Cold drinks—like the much-ballyhooed fresh-squeezed orange juice—were kept outside in a cooler. Managers made only $12/week, but lodging was part of the deal. As the locations were picked for their proximity to the highways—not to towns or any signs of civilization—living quarters were nestled in the back behind the snack counters.

Success that had dangled in front of Bigdaddy for years like the wind chimes in his stores was finally his. The future he imagined while farming cotton and grading pecan varieties had arrived. But then tragedy struck. On December 7, 1941, the Japanese bombed Pearl Harbor. America was at war. Everything changed in that instant.

Along with the devastating loss of lives, World War II also brought economic hard times. My grandfather was ineligible for service because of flat feet that caused him pain throughout his life, but he fought challenges of his own at home. Wartime rationing hit him hard. Suddenly, there was no sugar, no gas, no tourists. The essential ingredients for his business were gone. Even if he had been able to stock his stores with food and fuel, there were no vacations in Florida while Americans were fighting abroad. Everything came to a halt.

The Stuckey's in Folkston, Georgia, was the first casualty. It fell victim to bootleggers who broke into the store, stole the sugar for liquor, and set the place ablaze to cover their crime. My grandfather put his salesman skills to work to keep the two remaining stores open. Even in wartime, truck and bus drivers remained a mainstay on America's highways. Bigdaddy bartered scarce items like cigarettes, shotgun shells, and shoes to entice the drivers to pull over at his stores. It worked enough to keep Eastman afloat, although Unadilla also had to shutter its doors.

Hell-bent on surviving and with only one store remaining, Bigdaddy developed a cunning ability to swap anything for sugar—from nylon stockings to cottonseed meal and meat. He bragged that he had once traded fish guts for sugar. Whether it was true or not, he claimed at the time that he was one of the largest sugar brokers in the country, once trading Tom's candies in Atlanta one hundred thousand pounds of corn syrup for sixty thousand pounds of sugar. He even invested in a stick candy factory in Jacksonville, Florida, to get a larger quota of government-issued sugar. He skimped on how much sugar went into each pound of candy at the Jacksonville plant so he could divert most of it to his Eastman operations.

My favorite story about the lean war years is how my grandfather used his ingenuity—and a secret ingredient—to continue making his coconut patties. As the main ingredient was in short supply, Bigdaddy took artificial flavoring from the stick candy plant and mixed it with ground-up corn husks. This was before federal regulations requiring disclosure, thank goodness, so he was able to market his creative concoction as "genuine coconut patties." They were a hit, with customers lining up around the block to buy them, and no one the wiser as to how they were made.

Ultimately, though, it took more than trickery and trading to survive the war. Stuckey's salvation was the same strategy relied upon by most of America's candymakers, from Hershey's to M&M Mars: selling to the military. The best way to get sugar during that era—and help the wartime effort—was to provide rations for the troops. My grandfather scored a contract with the Department of Defense to make confections that supplied quick energy for men fighting on the front lines.

Before the war, all his candy had been made on-site in small batches in the store kitchens. He had no experience with mass production, packaging, or food preservation. Bigdaddy built a candy operation in his pecan warehouse in Eastman. The building was only 240 square feet, and he filled it with Coleman burners and a couple of boiling pots. But "it served its purpose," as he would later recount. By 1944, he was selling $150,000 worth of candy a year to the armed forces.

Resilience is the art of bouncing back; it's embracing challenge as an opportunity for reinvention. That's what my grandfather did to endure and even thrive during the war.

Manufacturing at scale was a game changer for Stuckey's. As the war came to a close, Bigdaddy put his new skills to use by packaging candy in attractive boxes. This opened a new sales channel for retail stores. He increased his prices—from a dollar for a two-pound bag of candy to half that amount in a box for the same price. It worked. He sold more candy than ever before.

Bigdaddy's eagerness to drive sales, unfortunately, led to a run-in with the Mafia. He got a big break at a candy convention in Atlanta: a large purchase order from Rich's department store. While the fighting had ceased, the rations continued. Ingredients like sugar were still in short supply and high demand. To fill the order, he needed to produce a lot of candy with a fast turnaround. He made some inquiries and located fifty thousand pounds of sugar from a guy he knew in Miami. Everything seemed to be falling into place. That is, until two agents from the Federal Bureau of Investigation showed up at his home in Eastman with questions about his sugar dealer. It turns out that he'd been trading in the black market with the Cuban mob who had extensive sugar connections. My grandfather told the authorities everything he knew, pleading that he wasn't making illegal booze but was "just a candy man." They let him go; he'd dodged a bullet. Bigdaddy later boasted that he was one of the few people to evade the law and the Mafia. The check he'd written to his Miami contact for the sugar was seized as evidence by the FBI and never cashed.

This inauspicious close to the war years was thankfully not an augur of things to come. Americans returning home held dear the freedoms they fought for on the battlefields of Europe and the Pacific front. As they settled down with jobs, mortgages, and families, their escape from the mundanity of their suburban lifestyle was to take a road trip. The highway was the only way to vacation in the mid-1940s. Airplanes and cruise ships were an unattainable luxury for all but an elite few. Beyond the practicality and affordability of travel by car was what the automobile represented to post-war America.

The road trip meant freedom in an era when daily life was restricted by social norms and career expectations. The ease of loading the family in a car and leaving stress in the rearview mirror is what led millions of families to take to the open road to explore America. They thought nothing of a three- or four-day drive from Massachusetts to Myrtle Beach. The journey was as adventurous as the destination.

Roadside attractions cropped up across the vernacular landscape—the repetition of lonely South Dakota fields broken by a corn palace in Mitchell or Gatorland punctuating a stretch of U.S. 441 in Florida. Often considered the first roadside oddity, Lucy the Elephant towered six stories above the highway south of Atlantic City's boardwalk. This was when wigwam motels and diners shaped like coffeepots ruled the road like conquering heroes, claiming their turf on highways across America.

It was an era when design mattered: from the sleek tail fins and hood ornaments of the everyday car to the polished chrome and blinking neon of diners. Billboards didn't just offer directions; they were art and entertainment. Burma-Shave signs parceled out morsels of stories like crumbs leading the drivers to their destination. South of the Border, a quirky stop that began as a beer depot, morphed into a purveyor of all things kitsch: from Mexican falsa blankets to back scratchers. Their signs kept bored back-seat kids amused for hours with hokey sayings like, "You Never Sausage a Place" and "Keep Yelling, Kids—They'll Stop."

My grandfather, full of cash and ambition, recognized this boom of roadside travel as his defining moment. The carnival ride of business highs interrupted by unexpected swerves he'd been on was finally coming to a halt. The war years had hit everyone hard; the home front was no exception. While not comparable to the intensity of the battlefield, he'd nonetheless braved financial hardships and emerged victorious. He'd built up a solid profit base from selling candy to the armed forces and the Rich's deal. Even though sugar rationing remained until 1947, he was undeterred, re-opening his Unadilla and Folkston stores in 1945. Stuckey's incorporated two years later and opened its first franchise in Sunny Side, Georgia. By 1948, he added a fifth location in Richmond Hill, south of Savannah.

As the road trip grew, so did Stuckey's, aligned with the greater mobility of the 1950s motoring public and roadway expansion. Southern routes, notably U.S. 17, 301, and 1, were thronged with automobiles. Stuckey's was a welcome respite for hordes of northern snowbirds flocking to Florida for their winter sojourns. At the time, Highway 1, which ran from Maine to Key West, was the most well-traveled road on the Eastern Seaboard, and Stuckey's populated it with its prom-ises of ice-cold drinks, tasty pecan treats, homemade sand-wiches, and fun souvenirs. Stuckey's caught on because there were no other businesses on the highways. In the 1950s, there were desolate stretches of asphalt; no one else was competing with what we offered.

In 1950, Bigdaddy invested in a refrigerated trailer to ensure that his candy cargoes arrived on time and in good condition. Within a few years, he grew this initial purchase into a sizable fleet of trucks, employing drivers to run routes to the ever-expanding locations.

By 1953, Stuckey's had multiplied to twenty-nine stores and was becoming a familiar sight along the roadways of the South, now stretching into Florida and South Carolina. This prosperity was a boon to Stuckey's hometown of Eastman.

On March 4 of that year, Bigdaddy cut the ribbon on a new $125,000 office building and candy plant on the McRae Highway. He persuaded the local public works office to pave a connector to the entrance. With its own road, the red brick complex was aptly designated as "100 Candy Court." Two years later, a $100,000 expansion was added.

Bigdaddy believed in community. Stuckey's offered an income and way of life for residents of Dodge County. He hired locals as employees: from the front lines in the candy plant to executives in the C-suites. Women and African Americans made up a good portion of the workforce—a practice begun during the war years out of necessity but that continued afterward as a matter of choice. Years later, a worker named Mary Alice Mullis recalled in a letter to my grandfather how Stuckey's offered women who had never worked outside the home ways to add to their family's income. "People of different race, different backgrounds, and opposite sexes found themselves on common ground as they worked side by side."

Admittedly, Stuckey's was not a Shangri-La of equality. There were barriers to promotion for women and minorities, as evidenced in the annual company portraits: row upon row of white men in suits. Yet, in the context of the times, it was more progressive than others, as my grandfather believed in elevating people as much as brick-and-mortar buildings. The product of the school of hard knocks himself, he did not insist that his executives have college degrees. He hired for character and trained his team on how to do their jobs.

My grandfather often rewarded his employees with an interest in the stores. The advantages to this were twofold:

It kept him cash flow positive and incentivized employees. Even workers in the machine shop, warehouse, and candy plant owned interests in the stores—men and women, Blacks and whites, were given shares in Stuckey's stores. His secretary, for example, only earned $75 a week, but she grossed $16,000 yearly from store proceeds.

The stores fared well because of their business model, one that Bigdaddy developed and honed with those first three stores before the war. The key to this model was the husband-and-wife team that managed the stores.

In exchange for seed money in the range of $50,000, the couple would reside in and run the store assigned to them. They signed a contract to sell only Stuckey's candy and merchandise and Texaco gasoline at the store. As most of the couples were young with limited savings, my grandfather usually bore the startup expenses himself. Stuckey's had a distribution center that sourced and sold the novelties to the stores for a profit. Company accountants managed the books for the stores to ensure that accounts were maintained correctly—and the owners were honest. All categories of merchandise were successful: sales of candy, snacks, souvenirs, and gasoline all turned a profit. Promotions, advertising, and displays were driven by company headquarters and filtered down to the store level. From top to bottom, operations ran like a well-oiled machine.

There were very few company-owned locations—only about ten. The remainder were run using this franchise model, with the husband-and-wife franchisees being the center of operations. Bigdaddy looked after them like family, remembering birthdays and special events in company news-letters and with personal cards. He encouraged the franchi-sees to add special touches to their stores to create a sense of ownership in the stores they ran. The fact that the stores were their homes no doubt added to the homey feel customers had when walking through the doors. It was not uncommon to see on the menu board some specialty the wife had made, like deviled eggs or pimento cheese. At the holidays, stores competed for the most festive decorations, stacking towers of pecan log rolls into trees adorned with stars and glitter.

The stores all had snack bars, not full-service restaurants. My grandfather was insistent that customers should be walk-ing around, buying candy and souvenirs, not seated at tables eating. He was frugal in all aspects of the business. Labor was the costliest line item on any budget, so he economized by not employing wait staff. Bigdaddy believed that the trav-eling public just wanted a quick, hot snack. Families on a budget didn't want to spend $10 for lunch when they stopped for gas. He was always thinking about the customer. Most service stations offered little other than crackers and soft drinks. Stuckey's with its snack bars presented the perfect in-between option—hot dogs, hamburgers, grilled cheese, and other simple fare made on-site. "Tasty food at a reason-able price" was his promise, and he kept it.

It was during this time that Bigdaddy launched one of his most successful pull-over-now ideas: the King of the Road breakfast special. Consisting of two eggs, toast, and jelly, it was known as a "loss leader" at ninety-nine cents a plate. It would draw in customers with its low price. Once in the store, the logic went, they would spend money on other products to make up for the initial loss. It was an instant hit and remains to this day a popular menu item.

This focus on personal touches paid off in immeasurable ways. My grandfather often received letters of appreciation from customers. One letter in his archives was from an Italian man, Anthony Tito, grateful for a store owner's return of his wife's lost wedding ring—free of charge. There was also correspondence from celebrities like Bob Hope and Bing Crosby, thanking Bigdadday for gifts of candy. My grandfather, ever the salesman, no doubt targeted the popular entertainers of the day to receive Stuckey's treats in hopes they'd offer free endorsements. He was ahead of his time in cultivating famous influencers for his products.

Bigdaddy also insisted that stores go out of their way to be friendly to travelers. He encouraged stores to clean customers' windshields. They would return to their cars with a note informing them that their clear view was courtesy of Stuckey's Pecan Shoppe. He also would have employees bring old cars to the store parking lots and keep them there, theorizing that a busy-looking store would attract more customers.

Bigdaddy was a restless man, rarely content to sit at his desk attending to paperwork. He would frequently make impromptu visits to his stores. He had a gift for remembering names and made a point of greeting everyone personally. That intensity applied equally to the customers. He would obsess over who his customers were to better meet their needs. Managers would frequently see him in the parking lot with a clipboard, tallying the license plates. He learned that much of his clientele were northern tourists from states like New York, New Jersey, and Pennsylvania, heading south to visit relatives in Florida. Bigdaddy especially was on the lookout for Ohio plates. He considered that to be a bellwether state and centrally situated. If customers were coming from Ohio, it was a harbinger that business was good.

My grandfather recognized that for many of our customers, pulling in at Stuckey's was their introduction to Southern culture, so he stressed to all his managers the importance of making a good first impression. They were ambassadors of the warmth and hospitality that defined our brand.

Walking into one of the stores was a feast for the eyes, with an array of displays piled high with trinkets, state souvenirs, and toys. The layout was deliberately maze-like, so customers were forced to wind their way through the myriad of wares before arriving at the restrooms or snack bar along the back wall. In between those two road stop essentials stood the pièce de résistance: the wall of candy. Metal letters in beautiful old-time font spanned the breadth of the space announcing "CANDIES" in all caps. Below were stacks of pralines, divinity, fudge, and the ever-present pecan log roll. The hapless tourist couldn't escape without being lured into the candy trap and taking home a bagful.

In reviewing my grandfather's papers, I repeatedly came across the saying "Every Traveler Is a Friend." As I read his stories and learned about how the company grew during this time, I could see how this mantra was reflected in every aspect of running the business. This was most evident by the fact that Stuckey's stores were never segregated. All were welcome. There were no "whites only" signs. Our stores being located outside most city limits helped—we were able to evade sundown town laws and other racially discriminatory ordinances. We also escaped notice with our stores designed for the in-and-out-traveler. Our customers were on the go and rarely stayed long enough to draw the attention of law enforcement or locals. My grandfather simply and quietly did the right thing. In fact, it wasn't until decades later—when Stuckey's was featured in a scene in *Green Book*, a film about road travel in the racially divided South—that I learned this aspect of our family's history. Of Bigdaddy's many achievements, it's this silent act of kindness and humanity that makes me the proudest.

Chapter 9

REMEMBER THE
HULA-HOOP

The franchise system that my grandfather built with husband-and-wife teams running the stores was profitable because the stores sourced 100 percent of their product through Stuckey's Distribution. Along with manufacturing, a billboard plant, and a trucking operation, Stuckey's vertically integrated model functioned extremely well.

By the time I took over, this seamless operation had long ceased to exist. There were only the thirteen original Stuckey's that remained on the nation's highways, plus about fifty of the hybrid store models. All that remained in Eastman was that rented warehouse about a mile down the road from 100 Candy Court where Stuckey's once thrived.

Margins were tight to run the warehouse—we had to add

a profit for our operations when sourcing from vendors, then the stores would get their markup. While we were switching to a business model focused on manufacturing our own product, we still needed the distribution model to stay afloat financially. Recurring income on a balance sheet, I quickly learned, is critical. The monthly automatic transfers from these store accounts helped us maintain cash flow. It was like a marriage of convenience where you stay together for the children and financial stability. The stores were Stuckey's children, and the modest fees we earned from the licensing and distribution program offered needed stability. We couldn't afford to leave and had to make the best of a difficult situation.

With R.G. running the plant in Wrens, much of the warehouse oversight shifted to me. I could stay at our family farm for free and enjoy a retreat from Atlanta, where COVID-19 restrictions remained largely in place.

As working remotely became more accepted during this time, there was less pressure for me to travel to Eastman every week. But I visited regularly and kept daily contact by phone and email, learning the ropes and identifying ways to improve efficiencies and profitability. While it's an obvious Business 101 strategy to cut costs and grow sales, execution is easier on paper than in real life.

We conducted what's known as a SKU rationalization whereby every item number is assessed for its gross margins, profitability, and sales volume. I added an additional factor of whether it was brand worthy. I worked with our designer to put together a style guide to set merchandising standards.

There's a fine line between tacky and kitsch, and—like the famous quote from Supreme Court justice Potter Stewart on pornography ("I know it when I see it")—I had an innate sense of what items were irreverent fun and which were just plain cheap. We did our best to elevate the brand, but ultimately it was a balance between the new image R.G. and I wanted for the company and what we could afford.

Some items were so cringeworthy that friends would text me photos from our stores with comments like "I can't believe you sell this." But customers bought them. For example, we sold thousands of resin figurines: Jesus on the cross, a wolf howling at the moon, or a foot-high rooster. I couldn't imagine displaying one in my home, but I'd sit in our stores and watch folks pay up to $49.99 for them.

"If it's tacky, it sells," is my father's taste barometer. "This isn't Neiman Marcus. We cater to all walks of life. Don't ever forget that." If an ashtray shaped like a toilet that says "put your butts here" made us money, then—at least for the time being—I would have to let my personal opinion take a back seat to sales.

The inventory review helped us weed out the clutter that wasn't moving from the items that were. That was the good news. The bad part is that we had $40,000 in dead inventory that was gathering dust. Stuff like three cases of Britney Spears T-shirts emblazoned with "Brittney Bitch," Polynesian sarongs, toothpick holders, redneck back scratchers, and hundreds of *High School Musical* flashing key chains. The deadest of the dead inventory, however, was the stack of boxes filled with fidget spinners. We had over ten thousand of the neon-colored gadgets that had been briefly popular in 2017. Whenever I thought we had a good count on their numbers, we would discover another case hidden behind a stack of old displays or under a desk in the warehouse office. They were like Tribbles in that famous *Star Trek* episode, multiplying with a life of their own.

It reminded me of a cautionary tale I had grown up hearing from my father. "Remember the Hula-Hoop," he would warn me with the same gusto as a Texan talking about the Alamo. Back in the early 1960s, Stuckey's purchased a truckload of the hip-swiveling popular toy at a good price, eager to cash in on the latest craze. Unfortunately, like pet rocks, Garbage Pail Kids, Rubik's Cubes, and slap bracelets, all good fads come to an end—and usually way too soon for the vendors who get stuck with the excess inventory. "Your grandfather couldn't give those things away," my father reminisced, shaking his head. "Remember the Hula-Hoop and the fidget spinner" would become my battle cry moving forward, a warning not to be revisited by the ghosts of our retail past. A lesson had been learned. But that didn't negate the pallets full of the stress-relieving toy that ironically invoked constant anxiety.

We had recently hired a new warehouse manager named Rickey Mathis who'd spent his career working logistics for a large corporation. He was friends and former colleagues with Vicki Cannington. The two of them were indispensable in organizing the dead inventory we had accumulated over the years. We segregated all the slow SKUs to one section, initially allocating only a few racks but soon taking over an entire section of the warehouse with rows and rows of state souvenirs, postcards, Coca-Cola drinking cups, *Frozen* Disney plates, metal "man cave" signs, salt and pepper shakers, and the ubiquitous fidget spinners.

This inventory was so dead, it was off life support and had flatlined. Even liquidation firms that brokered in junk weren't interested. I considered setting up a tent in downtown Eastman to unload the cheap wares, throwing in a free pecan log roll with every purchase. I was willing to brave the ignominy of such a feat—with locals gossiping about how far the Stuckey's had fallen—but the math didn't work. It'd cost more for tent rental, time, and labor than the likely profits. Then, a childhood memory offered a solution.

Whenever we stopped at Stuckey's on road trips, my dad would give me and my four siblings a few bucks each. The business was no longer ours, so it wasn't like we could roam the aisles grabbing stuff for free. But the sign out front still bore our name and a sense of pride. It was the highlight of our family vacations.

My brothers loved pop guns and rubber tomahawks; my sister the coloring books. But my favorite purchase was found in a bargain dump bin. It was filled with white- and turquoise-striped sacks with "Mystery Bag" printed on them in black ink. They were a buck apiece and stuffed with knickknacks. They had been another one of my grandfather's brainstorms. He bundled up random items that weren't selling into these mystery bags—toenail clippers, pencil sharpeners, plastic jewelry, lollipops, you name it. All found a haven and a second life repurposed in those bags. Some contained nicer, pricer items; others were cheap trinkets. But that was the mystery and beauty of them.

Like a sequel to a blockbuster movie, the mystery bag could be a hit again. Although instead of paper bags, we used our Stuckey's display boxes. We had cases of them, and they were sturdy enough to hold the various items. I built a workspace of stacked pallets topped with cardboard and assembled a hundred Mystery Boxes, pricing them at $24.99 apiece. I'd make a profit of $3–5 per unit, 20 percent or less, but still better than taking up space on our shelves.

I snapped a photo on my iPhone holding up a John Wayne bobblehead in one hand and a yellow box filled with assorted goodies in the other. I used this image to format an e-blast to the few thousand customers we had in our system, announcing the return of the Stuckey's Mystery Gift. I set up a tripod at the warehouse and shot a video of me assembling boxes that I posted on LinkedIn, Instagram, Facebook, and TikTok. In my fifties, I'm self-conscious about my wrinkles and age. But the reality is that we couldn't afford a twenty-something social media influencer wearing a low-cut dress. We would have to make do with selfies of me, a middle-aged CEO, wearing a Stuckey's sweatshirt. If Orville Redenbacher and Dave Thomas could rep their brands, why couldn't I? We all had the same thing going for us: authenticity. After I finished my round of Mystery Box posts, I said a silent prayer that the Bigdaddy mojo was still alive and shut my computer off. Nothing to do but wait and hope.

By the next afternoon, the WooCommerce dashboard for our website was showing a handful of Mystery Boxes had sold. This gave me a confidence nudge, and I did another round of emails and social media posts. The Mystery Boxes sales grew exponentially. So much so that I spent most of my time between Black Friday and Christmas at the warehouse building Mystery Boxes and filling online orders. I even recruited friends like Jamie Allen, a freelance writer who was helping manage our email communications, and his buddy Stewart Haddock to haul down to Eastman for the day to work in the warehouse. Jamie showed me how to do my first live video as we threw random items in yellow boxes, with Stewart narrating in a funny, deadpan tone. I was amazed that over a hundred folks joined us online and posted encouraging comments about the Stuckey's comeback.

By the close of the year, the Mystery Boxes were surpassed only by the pecan log roll in number of units sold. We had made over $50,000 in profit on dead inventory that we initially had considered writing off and taking a financial hit. I learned a lot of lessons while helping manage the warehouse operations, but the most important one was that when life gives you lemons, you make lemonade. Or, in my case, when life gives you slap bracelets, fidget spinners, and Britney Bitch T-shirts, you make Mystery Boxes.

Chapter 10

EVERY TRAVELER
IS A FRIEND

By the mid-1950s, my grandfather's roadside dominance had spread up and down the Eastern Seaboard and begun to venture west. Life was good, and business was booming. Then, as with the bombing of Pearl Harbor, crisis struck. This time, it wasn't a foreign threat but a domestic one instigated by the president of the United States.

In 1956, President Eisenhower announced the construction of a national highway system. This promised to streamline travel and make the transport of goods more efficient. Inspired by the German autobahn with its fast-speed network of roads, Eisenhower viewed this massive public works project as critical to national security as well as economic prosperity. The "Big I" promised to transform tumbleweed towns like Albuquerque, Denver, and Phoenix into commercial hubs, a pathway of prosperity linking America.

But there was a cost to this, extracted from those who could least afford to pay. Communities, most of them minority and disadvantaged, were sacrificed in the guise of progress and planning. Buildings, homes, and dreams were demolished across the country, viewed as an unavoidable by-product of innovation.

Also erased were the blue lines on maps that once pulsed with cars like veins giving life to small towns. As if a callous engineer had knocked over a row of dominoes on a road atlas, businesses across America fell in rapid succession. Down went motor courts with "refrigerated air," tiled bathrooms, and coin-operated radios. Fallen by the wayside were railcar diners, empty booths that once framed hungry travelers lined against the windows. A giant fiberglass statue cradling a hot dog was left idle at a closed snack bar along Route 66. The colorful pageantry of roadside Americana was bypassed in favor of fast-moving corridors of asphalt and convenience.

Stuckey's had been part of this world, our stores with talking birds and coconut head statutes were located alongside petting zoos and fiberglass dinosaur parks. It had been a profitable symbiosis, but our coexistence began to crumble when many of these attractions closed.

My grandfather was faced with a critical decision: stand his ground with the drive-ins and trading posts or relocate to the bleak bulldozed turnoffs along the new interstate. He chose to survive—but on his terms. Moving was unavoidable. Yet his stores could offer a break from the ho-hum sameness that would now occupy the roadside landscape. This crisis could quite possibly be his big break.

Once he made a decision, there was no turning back. Unlike other businesses that stuck their proverbial flags in the ground along the soon forgotten routes, Stuckey's embraced the reality of the interstate and used it as an opportunity for improvement.

Chief among these was the siting of the stores. Bigdaddy knew where every stretch of the new highway was going. He deployed his advance team to state departments of transportation to dig through records and road histories. As if on an espionage mission, the Stuckey's spies were known to sweet talk secretaries and lavish highway officials with cases of pecan log rolls in exchange for information.

Armed with knowledge and maps, Bigdaddy became an astute real estate broker. He would walk onto a field that produced $50 worth of cotton a year and offer $6,000 an acre. The surprised farmer figured he was taking a city slicker for a ride. A year later, however, a new interstate would slice through the property, and a blue Stuckey's roof would crop up where cotton had once grown. Bigdaddy joked that he financed so many Cadillacs for farmers during that time that he should've gotten a commission.

My grandfather was very particular about where his stores were built, down to the side of the road they occupied. He theorized that the right side of the highway heading north was the more profitable side; the logic being that families were less likely to spend money heading south to Florida. They would be inclined to save their funds for their vacation, plus wouldn't want to haul packages around. Folks heading north after vacation were better prospects, so the Stuckey's stores would be waiting for them conveniently on the right side of the road. Bigdaddy also preferred stores on elevated ground that were visible for miles or along a curve where drivers had to slow down.

Bigdaddy was conflicted about divided highways. He liked that they were softer and well-paved. But they made it hard to do a U-turn if a traveler passed a Stuckey's. Everything was centered around the driving experience, making it easy for his customers to pull over. To test his various theories, he personally conducted surveys of northbound versus southbound traffic and watched how cars pulled in and out of his parking lots. Were they coming from in state or out of state, loaded up with luggage or packing light for a business trip? All of this mattered and exposed a man obsessed with succeeding, of never again inhaling exhaust as cars sped by his roadside stand.

Perhaps the most revealing story about his character is how Bigdaddy calculated the distance between Stuckey's locations. He would start driving on the interstate with a cup full of coffee. When nature called him to pull over, that's how far apart he'd place his stores. If only I had been in the car with him on those store siting trips. He would've built double the number of stores, and perhaps our fate would have been different.

Whether this is the stuff of family lore or not, what I know to be true is that Bigdaddy was a master observer of human behavior. Knowing what people want and giving it to them is the essence of entrepreneurship. He had a gift for that. More than the products he sold or the services he offered, that innate sense of empathy is what made him rich.

In today's competitive business environment, where an MBA from a prestigious college is a prerequisite to most C-suite jobs, this is sadly often overlooked. I was recently meeting with professionals with decades of education and experience developing convenience stores. They were pitching a modern Stuckey's concept.

The stores, they explained, would be sited at key intersections based on how many miles today's average car can drive on a full tank of gas. The store layouts they had drafted showed the bathrooms right at the entrance. I could almost see Bigdaddy shaking his head at their proposal.

Anyone who has driven with children knows you stop when they need to go, not when your tank is empty. Bigdaddy's coffee method stands the test of time. And a store designed to facilitate quick in-and-out trips to the restroom instead of navigating through rows of merchandise does little to drive sales.

What rang up the most sales for Stuckey's, though, was not inside at the register but outside at the pump. Gas was the big-ticket item. And the deal he brokered with Texaco is what made him a millionaire. Prior to the Interstate, my grandfather sourced gas for his stores from a variety of oil companies. Once Stuckey's started establishing a consistent presence on America's highways, Bigdaddy figured he could parlay this dominance to his advantage. He pitched to Texaco that they could be the exclusive gas brand sold at his stores.

Their familiar red star alongside Stuckey's equally recognizable logo, he argued, would be welcome sight for road-weary travelers. Texaco agreed. Stuckey's rolled out a new slogan, "Relax, Refresh, Refuel," to elevate the importance of gas among their offerings, a one-stop shop where all your pull-over needs were met.

Credit: Stuckey's Archives

Embracing Change: My grandfather celebrated moving
to the interstate, even though it was challenging for his business.
This postcard captures how he looked for the positive,
like finding an asphalt highway beautiful.

The partnership worked. Stuckey's became synonymous with Texaco. My grandfather negotiated what he called "a sweetheart deal." He personally pocketed a twenty-five-cent profit on every gallon of gas sold. With the stores pumping forty thousand gallons of gas a month, that made him a fortune. Stuckey's also benefited from Texaco having one of the first credit cards that was rolled out nationwide. This proved to be a nice incentive as Stuckey's expanded to over forty states and became one of the largest retailers of Texaco gas in the United States.

As the American road trip evolved, my grandfather evolved with it. Reading his story fifty years later gave me a map as I struggled to rebuild his life's work. He left me with me two lessons in resilience—surviving World War II and the bypassing of his stores. Like him, I would have to learn to let go of what wasn't working and embrace change. And like him, I—along with R.G. and our team—were determined we were going to make it.

Chapter 11

THE ART OF
THE SIDE HUSTLE

By late 2021, it'd been over two years since I had sunk my life's savings into buying Stuckey's. While I had set aside some funds for my living expenses, my financial runway was running out. I had quit eating out, buying new clothes, and taking vacations. We shopped at Goodwill and cooked dinners at home. But my bank account was dipping precariously low.

True, my parents were wealthy; I could go to them with my hand out. Yet, my father's words that I couldn't even run a lemonade stand had struck me where it hurt the most: my pride. I'd rather continue driving a junky car and wearing sneakers with flopping soles than admit to Dad that times were tough.

So, I did what Bigdaddy did: I got a couple of side hustles.

I first rented out my house as an Airbnb. Living in the heart of Atlanta near the BeltLine and the trendy Little Five Points shopping district, my listing booked quickly. I made $150/night, not enough to live off of but a welcome addition to my income.

I picked up a second unexpected gig: public speaking. As COVID-19 restrictions were lessening and people started holding events again, I was offered a keynote slot at a convening of over four hundred prominent businesspeople in Atlanta. I was so flattered that it didn't occur to me to request an honorarium. I spent weeks preparing and hired Jamie, the freelancer who had been helping with Stuckey's communications, as my coach. I practically memorized the talk to ease my nerves. But when it came time to stand in front of the large audience, I found that telling the story of the Stuckey's revival and the lessons learned was easy to share. I was honest that we were still struggling on our comeback journey, but folks appreciated the authenticity. Word-of-mouth referrals led to more invitations, this time for money. As my confidence grew, so did my fees, generating $50,000 by year's end.

My brothers especially find it amusing that I get paid to speak, as they would have paid me to shut up when we were kids. But the timing was perfect to share a feel-good message that comebacks are possible as our country and businesses were recovering from the pandemic. I was grateful to share our story and meet others who were passionate about family businesses, small-town America, road tripping, and manufacturing, giving keynote addresses at conferences like Stand Up for Rural America, Route 66 Miles of Possibility, Florida Truckers Association, Georgia Community Bankers, and the Kitchen Cabinet Manufacturers.

Having a side hustle as an entrepreneur gives you an edge and keeps you grounded. I remember one day I was pitching Stuckey's to a potential investor on a video call. I had my hair styled conservatively and wore a blazer with a scarf tied around my neck. But below the desk, I had on jeans and flip flops. I looked at the clock and realized it was check-in time for my Airbnb. "I have another meeting scheduled and have to sign off now," I said crisply as if I had others waiting to be dazzled with our company's financial prospects. Instead, I rushed to pull linens out of the dryer and scrub toilets before my guests arrived. I wonder how they would have reacted if they knew all that I was juggling. Would they have admired my chutzpah and accepted that comebacks take time, or rejected Stuckey's as too much of a gamble for their risk-adverse clientele?

I suspect the latter, having been jaded by my dealings with potential investors, all of whom asserted they were "not like other private equity firms." Yet, they were all exactly alike, adhering to cookie-cutter formulas for success and devoid of creativity. One offered to buy a majority of the company for a fraction of what I thought Stuckey's was worth. I was speechless, which gave him an opening to add that they would need, of course, "to hire a real CEO."

"That would be a pass for me," I responded without

pause, more taken aback by his lack of tact than candor. To paraphrase a favorite Southern saying, "Bless his black Wall Street heart."

R.G. and I would have to grow Stuckey's the old-fashioned way—with hard work, sales, and traditional loans from community banks, just like my grandfather had. Like everything he did, relationships were what mattered. Bigdaddy relied on local banks to capitalize his growth. I didn't realize until I was grown that many of his friends that regularly visited his home for cocktails were his lenders. Every year, he hosted a Bankers Weekend on St. Simons Island, inviting his creditors to a relaxing time at the beach. My father continued this tradition with his own Bankers Weekend, only he added a financial briefing to review how their money had been used to drive growth and profitability. As we revive Stuckey's, I aim to continue this tradition of treating your bankers as your friends and partners in building your business and community.

As the facility in Wrens increased production—this time, thankfully, with new, odorless packaging—we expanded the number of stores that carried the Stuckey's brand. Our strategy was shifting from selling outsourced product that we paid others to make to selling our own manufactured snacks and candies to third-party retailers. We acquired these accounts by a variety of means, from working trade shows to cold calling via LinkedIn—plus, we had kept the extensive roster of Atwell Pecans' clients as part of the buyout deal. We had a small but mighty team of three sales representatives who serviced the legacy Stuckey's stores. As we transitioned to more of a consumer packaged goods company, they were encouraged to land more outside accounts.

There was also the intricate system of brokers and distributors, a world as foreign to me as deciphering financial reports had been when I first bought the company. R.G. fortunately had run a wholesale business with his Front Porch Pecans. He schooled me on how these entities functioned to bring sweet and salty snacks to our nation's food aisles, a world we hope to dominate one day.

Brokers cultivate relationships with retailers to get your product on the shelves, often specializing in channels like grocery, convenience stores, gift shops, etc. In exchange, they charge a commission fee, usually 5–10 percent of sales (or higher). Distributors, unlike brokers, purchase your product up front and resell to stores, marking up the price to take their cut (usually 20–30 percent). They also tack on set up fees and slotting charges.

There's a reason why we see so few small brands make it to our snack aisles, especially ones owned by women or minorities. Every inch of shelf space is fought for and paid for. A new bag of chips discovered among the big, national brands is the result of years of hard work. Once your product lands in a spot, the battle for consumers' attention is just beginning. Every month, stores analyze their gross profit by SKU. The worst performing SKUs get "discoed"— not boogeying to eighties music but discontinued. The banished snacks get sent back to where they came from, their manufacturer forced to pay a credit for returned items. That's your parting gift as a losing contestant in the game of "Let's Sell Your Product." What's amazing is not that some unknown CPG brands manage to make it on the food shelves of America. What's amazing is that any make it there at all.

I don't hate brokers or distributors, but I am realistic that the system is inherently biased. I'll give an example. I was at a cocktail party hosted by one of our brokers at the Sweets and Snack trade show. Stuckey's had just gotten turned down by a major chain that I thought was a great fit for us. I spent most of the evening tracking down the broker who represented us at the pitch meeting with the retail chain. I finally found her chatting with a group of colleagues. She looked to be in her twenties. "Why wasn't Stuckey's selected for the account?" I asked. The young woman stared blankly, like a student who'd been caught unprepared for class. "I'm sorry," she said, gulping a swig of champagne. "What is Stuckey's?" "That's my company," I shot back, my hands shaking. "You represent us. I've poured everything into reviving this brand, and you don't know who we are?" I held my gaze as the others shifted uncomfortably. "The whole pitch was only a few minutes long," she replied defensively. "They went with the big-name brands. I did my best." "Really?" I asked. "Well then, your best is not good enough. Stuckey's is more than a brand, it's a story. It's my story. Next time you go into a pitch meeting, you should know the story behind the brand, not just its price points and margin structure. It's the story that matters." I walked off, doubting that the woman or anyone else heard me.

The small brands, we're the party crashers, the ones who have to barge in on conversations, be impolite, and throw a fit to be noticed. Is it worth it? You bet. There is nothing more rewarding than walking in a store and seeing your product on the shelves.

One of my favorite moments like this occurred in a small town in New Mexico. I was taking Robert and Beverly on a Route 66 road trip for spring break. We were in Tucumcari, an oasis in the vast stretch of asphalt and desert between Amarillo and Albuquerque. Although it only has a population of 5,200, Tucumcari is a must-stop destination, a trip in the way-back machine to when roadside motels featured mid-century modern architecture and museum-worthy neon signage.

After a long stretch of driving, I had spent a restless night at the Roadrunner Lodge. I couldn't relax on this vacation, feeling overwhelmed by the challenges of getting our product to market. Even the "Magic Fingers" vibrating beds that brought back wonderful childhood memories failed to lull me to sleep. I decided to explore the town in the early morning light. It was the perfect time of day to take photos of places like the Motel Safari, its colorful sign out front still lit and the lobby filled with camel figurines. Across the street, the Blue Swallow Motel glowed in the morning light, a '53 powder blue Hudson parked below its iconic neon sign. As I was walking along the beautifully restored motor court rooms of the Blue Swallow, a blinking sign across the street caught my eye.

It belonged to Teepee Curios, a giant wigwam tourist shop. The building was brightly decorated with Native American images. And then I saw it—painted in bright red on the front were the words "We sell Stuckey's candy." Wow. I shook my head and smiled. A teepee trading post in the middle of the desert advertising Stuckey's candy. It lifted my spirits when I needed it the most. It was like my grandfather telling me to keep going, that everything would be OK.

I talked the kids into staying in town until the store opened. Road trips, I insisted, are about not being on a schedule. That logic, plus breakfast at Dell's Diner, convinced them to stay in Tucumcari a little longer. When Teepee Curios opened, we met the owner, Gar Engman, and his wife, who had run the place for a decade. They had moved to Tucumcari from Iowa and lovingly restored this former gas station. The place was a wonderful smorgasbord of memorabilia and fun. It was the highlight of our trip.

While we need the revenue and recognition we get from large retail chains, it's the mom-and-pop stores across America, like TeePee Curios, that I love. Seeing a Stuckey's pecan log roll in an unexpected place is like running into an old friend in a foreign city—you feel excited and grateful to make these chance encounters.

Credit: Stuckey's Archives

With Gar Engman. He and his wife, Heidi, have owned
and operated the historic Tee Pee Curios since 1985.

Beverly snapped a photo of me with Gar holding up a
pecan log roll. I look at it whenever I hit a slump. It reminds me that the entrepreneurial journey is about being
alone together. Starting or reviving a business can be very
isolating, but we're not alone. There are hundreds of Gars
across this country that are on this journey with us—and
us with them.

Credit: Stephanie Stuckey

A Sign When I Needed It Most: Coming across the Tee Pee Curios advertisement for Stuckey's in the small town of Tucumcari, NM, gave me hope in a low moment.

Chapter 12

BLUE ROOFS &
BILLBOARDS

Buildings should tell a story, not just house people and things. Good design is everything; my grandfather understood that. The architecture of his Stuckey's stores was the external ambassador for his brand. He spent years experimenting, evolving from his early box-shaped stores to later A-framed ones, each time adding different design elements to see what worked.

The move to the interstate was a chance to hit the reset button. After years of having a variety of store designs, he could adopt a consistent and easily identifiable architectural look for Stuckey's. An added boost was the post-war construction boom, which offered cheap labor and materials to build his stores. Bigdaddy started a construction firm and hired a young man named Russell Dean "RD" Franklin to head up real estate development. Franklin's son would later marry his daughter, my aunt Lynda, further cementing the close relationship they would form.

The store design that the two men created would come to define the Stuckey's brand. It had a signature architectural feature: the steep gabled roof. The soaring arch above the flatness of the highway stood out; it's what caught the eye after hours of bleary sameness on the highways. The color was also attention grabbing. Bigdaddy selected its distinctive teal to contrast with the dull gray of asphalt. As if shouting, "Look at me, too," the tall pole sign bore a splashy Stuckey's logo in red and yellow. A new, sleeker Stuckey's logo was launched with the move to the interstate, more streamlined like the automobiles of the day. The logo's color combination was carefully chosen. Red grabs attention like a vibrant traffic sign urging motorists to pull over while yellow evokes happiness and warmth. Together they promise that fun lies ahead if you just turn on your blinkers and exit now. It's no surprise that the most successful fast-food chains employ the same colors and tactics. McDonald's, Burger King, In-N-Out, and others all use mustard and ketchup yumminess in their branding palette.

Motorists were also greeted with a playful zigzag car canopy. Unlike the ho-hum of today's flat and utilitarian canopies, the ones at Stuckey's were created to celebrate the automobile and freedom. This was the era when gas stations were known for their form as much as their function, like the elegant Phillips 66 gulf wing coverings that soared skyward. Going for a ride—whether a Sunday outing or a family vacation—was meant to be an experience, and my grandfather treated it as such.

When mom or dad pulled over at a Stuckey's, car-weary kids would find mechanical horse rides waiting out front for a quarter to bring them to life. The glass-doored vestibule gave them a glimpse of what awaited them inside. These breezeways served a practical function during inclement weather. But they also housed gumball machines and wooden stands stuffed with travel brochures for exotic attractions like Weeki Wachee, Citrus Tower, and Gatorland.

Yet this was all prelude to the big aha moment. When they walked into the store, visitors would ooh and aah at the vaulted ceiling that stretched a full two stories. Chandeliers more befitting a fine home hung from the rafters. My grandfather was inspired by an upside-down ship's hull for this flamboyant look, so completely unexpected in a roadside store. It's a testament to how he saw the world. He took a dull and necessary occurrence—pulling over for gas and using the restroom—and made it a beautiful adventure.

It was always all about the customer. As expected after a long car ride, families would typically head straight to the bathrooms. But this destination was only reached after weaving through displays piled high with pecan treats and novelties, with the center of attention being the mirrored wall of candy adjacent to the ladies' and men's rooms. Rarely would a traveler survive this gauntlet without an insatiable desire to take home a souvenir state plate, beaded necklaces, Adams magic tricks, Foster Grant sunglasses, or a pecan log roll.

The entire layout of the stores facilitated the needs of the traveler. Stuckey's ads promised their customers affordable "hurry-up snacks." Meals were hot dogs, pimento cheese sandwiches, and fresh hamburgers grilled in minutes. The ideal road fare for my grandfather was something that could be eaten by hand while meandering through his towers of tchotchkes. Very limited seating was offered for this reason. He didn't want customers at a table when they could be browsing and buying. Food service offered slim margins; his money was to be made in gas, candy, and what he affectionately referred to as "trash and trinkets." The more pet rocks and name drop leather bracelets with the 100 percent markup he sold, the better.

A brief narrative detour is warranted to apologize to some of our customers. Throughout my life, I've heard complaints from the Cassidys, Zoes, Tobiases, and Baxters of the world who've searched Stuckey's aisles in vain for a key chain, necklace, frame, or plastic purse with their name, while their friends named Amy, Holly, Robert, and Tom had a myriad of choices. I've long suspected that some parents who chose unusual names for their offspring were motivated by frugality as much as originality, knowing they'd be spared a lifetime of begging for tacky souvenirs.

Aside from the occasional disappointment of the Xaviers and Penelopes of the world, most visitors relished their childhood encounters with Stuckey's schlock—Wooly Willy, road trip bingo, Mad Libs, and Yes & Know books that they associate with our brand. To this day, random strangers will approach me in airports and ask where they can find a dunkin' bird toy. The sourcing of these eclectic curios was part of a deliberate brand strategy. The consistent items found in all store locations were toys intended to entertain bored back-seat children mixed with the pecan candies we made. And then there was the local fare the stores offered.

Bigdaddy had made significant concessions to his branding when he moved to the interstate. Gone were the slower-paced drives through towns like Winslow, Arizona, or Sullivan, Missouri, where windshield views offered a sense of place. A cotton field or a pine forest speeding by were the only clues of your whereabouts. For many tourists, these interludes at Stuckey's formed their understanding of Southern culture. Our stores offered a glimpse into small-town America for city slickers from New York, Philadelphia, and Chicago.

To restore some of what was lost in the move to exits off I-40, I-75, and more, my grandfather encouraged his managers to add unique local touches to their stores. For example, if you were taking a trip through Southern California in Palm Springs and pulled over at a Stuckey's, you would find date shakes on the menu with dates sourced from neighboring farmers. One of my favorite photographs of a Stuckey's was posted by a connection on LinkedIn. It shows him as a young boy, smiling with a date milkshake mustache, seated with his mom and siblings outside a Stuckey's. His mom is sporting stylish cat-eye sunglasses, and a John F. Kennedy key chain display is visible through the window behind them. Even though he's not in the picture, I can almost see my grandfather there, smiling at the sense of fun captured in that moment.

Credit: Stuckey's Archives

"Earl": The only clue to the fisherman's identity is "Earl" scrawled on the back of this undated photo found in my grandfather's archives. I posted it in a caption contest online, and the winning entry was "This is what you get when you use pecan log rolls as bait."

Another treasured image that I found in the Stuckey's archives is a man identified in cursive on the back as "Earl." He's got a big grin on his face, matched in size by the fish held in front of his puffed-up chest. Behind him is the familiar wall of candy stacked in neat rows. While the location isn't given, the photo was almost certainly snapped at one of the Stuckey's on the Gulf Coast that catered to a fishing clientele. These stores were stocked with the usual trinkets and pecan treats but also with lures, buckets of bait, and even fishing licenses. Folks would gather after a full day on the water and brag about their catches. I posted the photo on the Stuckey's Facebook page as part of a caption contest. The winning entry read, "This is what you get when you use pecan log rolls as bait."

The connection to the town beyond the nondescript exit marker was evident at Stuckey's from I-95 on the East Coast to I-10 across Texas. If you pulled over in Virginia, you'd find shelves full of Virginia peanuts and cured hams hanging on the walls. Stores in Texas had cowboy hats, boots, and toy pop guns. The Stuckey's employee newsletter, *Sweet Talk*, would highlight exemplary displays every month, inviting a friendly competition between store managers to have theirs featured in the next issue.

This receptiveness to novel ideas percolating from the store level is a mark of an effective leader. Some of the most profitable innovations in franchise history came from folks who worked on the front lines. The Big Mac, for example, was first introduced in 1967 by Jim Delligatti, a McDonald's franchisee in Uniontown, Pennsylvania. The brains behind Dairy Queen's famous blizzard was Samuel Temperato, who owned sixty-seven DQ locations and came up with the idea in 1985 as an alternative to a competitor's frozen custard dish. And Kentucky Fried Chicken can thank local store owner Pete Harman for its notorious bucket concept. Reportedly, Colonel Sanders asked Harman in 1957 to buy five hundred paper buckets he had in excess inventory. Harman found a use for them, filling each bucket with fifteen pieces of chicken, five rolls, and a pint of gravy, the perfect size for a take-home family meal. That red-and-white bucket became synonymous with the KFC brand and a top seller for decades.

While not as profitable as these staples of American fast food, one Stuckey's concept that is legendary in our history was likewise the brainstorm of a store owner. Unfortunately, his name is lost to time, but this anonymous marketing genius would lure customers into his store with a talking mynah bird. The sassy creature picked up a variety of phases like, "Corky wants a log roll." A feature in *Sweet Talk* created a multiplier effect with stores across the country adding a mynah bird to their repertoire of entertainment alongside vending machines and free fudge samples. Before Walmart had its vest-clad greeters, Stuckey's was ahead of its time with its fast-talking birds dishing out witty sayings.

I remember Corky, who was the resident mynah at the Eastman Stuckey's. Feeding her pieces of saltine crackers was the highlight of any trip to visit my grandfather. I searched through our records to find a photo of the bird, but the best I could muster was a blurry image accompanying a *Sweet Talk* story about foreign visitors. The article relayed that a group of Indians were touring our country and had stopped at a Stuckey's for a classic American experience. The family is clustered around a caged mynah bird looking completely uninterested, their young daughter staring off in the distance as if she wished she were anywhere else.

The United States Travel Service is bringing additional dollars into your store. Let's be extra nice to our Foreign Visitors.

Credit: Stuckey's Archives

Mynah Bird

I was surprised at their reaction given that most children's faces were filled with glee when seeing the talking birds. Then I realized what had been captured on film. Mynah birds are native to India. This family had trekked across the globe for a foreign experience only to see a bird as common to them as a pigeon is to Americans. Despite their lack of enthusiasm, I treasure the photo of the Indian tourists as the only record that remains of the talking mynah birds.

This spawned other store-led gimmicks, including cultivating beehives on-site that made fresh honey for customers. Sadly, health departments put an end to these stunts, but they remain in our company annals as a testament to the ingenuity of our frontline operators.

Another marketing program during this time was featuring small-town beauty queens in Stuckey's ads. My grandfather came up with this to celebrate the places where our stores are located. He used models like the Vidalia Onion

Princess and Miss Keep Dodge County Green (a title my mother once held). Having Miss Gum Spirits of Turpentine pose with display of Stuckey's candy would make the residents of Valdosta, Georgia, swell with hometown pride—and hopefully also buy pecan log rolls.

Credit: Stuckey's Archives

Beauty Queens: Bigdaddy loved to use local beauty queens to advertise his candy. I love this picture with the stereotypical Southern sheriff in the background smoking his cigarette and the young boy staring at the women.

Some folks may make fun of beauty queens, but in the South especially, it's ingrained in our culture and a part of who we are. As a teenager, I was crowned Miss Georgia Cherry Blossom, an accolade I kept on my resume until my law school counselor advised against it as unprofessional. I now disagree. Having reigned as Miss Cherry Blossom, I learned the importance of walking with confidence and poise, having a talent to entertain folks at boring cocktail parties (for the record, I can tap dance), and being OK with standing in front of a crowd. My pageant was more civic-minded and sponsored by the Georgia State Society, but the experience was invaluable in teaching me good posture and manners, essential life skills that are often overlooked. There are still moments to this day when I feel myself slumping in my chair that I can hear the pageant official scolding me to sit up straight and smile.

While the passage of time and advancement in women's rights has changed how society views beauty pageants, the fact remains that my grandfather had an innate talent to create a sense of place and belonging. From the local delicacies like date shakes to talking birds and beehives, Stuckey's was a roadside sanctuary that celebrated small-town America and broke the tedium of the highway.

In between our stores, the endless miles of road were punctuated by billboards that entertained as much as they informed.

The trailblazer in this form of advertising was Burma-Shave. Founded in Minneapolis in 1925, the company offered a brushless shaving cream. Sales were sluggish, so the owner's son, Allan Odell, came up with a campaign that used a series of small signs with rhyming slogans. The first one debuted in 1926 along Hwy 65 in Lakeville, Minnesota.

Allan wrote the clever sayings himself. Sales increased so much that Burma-Shave became the #2 shaving cream in the country. And seven thousand Burma-Shave signs stretched across America, becoming as essential to road trip entertainment as guessing games and singing. Sadly, the Burma-Shave ads fell victim to the interstate, abandoned by the wayside as car travel moved to the new venue.

My grandfather was likely inspired by Odell's clever prose and chutzpah, as well as other campaigns that followed suit, such as South of the Border, started in 1949 by Alan Schafer as a beer depot in Dillon, South Carolina. It fared better than many of its counterparts, surviving the construction of I-95 since it was conveniently located alongside the new highway. Schafer's business steadily expanded to include trinkets imported from Mexico, fireworks stands, and diversions like a go-kart track, putt-putt course, and a giant Sombrero Observation Tower. While the attractions were certainly a draw, what motivated generations of weary parents to pull over at South of the Border was its endless procession of billboards.

"Keep Yelling, Kids—They'll Stop," prompted one sign. Many rely on silly puns—like an enormous fiberglass salami with the phrase, "You Never Sausage a Place. (You're Always a Weiner at South of the Border.)" This slice of Americana survives to this day, along with its quirky billboards (although their cartoonish Mexican denizen, Pedro, has been replaced by a more culturally appropriate cactus mascot).

Road trips and billboards went together back then as

much as the Super Bowl and television ads today. It's no co-incidence, I think, that the attractions with the most clever and omnipresent billboards are still around, their advertising campaign a key to their longevity. Places like Wall Drug that offered "free ice water" with signs starting hundreds of miles away, have birthed hundreds of copycats posting photos of themselves in foreign places holding "Wall Drug—4,532 miles" signs. Other classics include "See Rock City" in Tennessee, The Thing in Arizona, and The Big Texan in Amarillo offering a "Free 72 oz. Steak Dinner" if eaten in less than an hour.

My grandfather hopped aboard the advertising band-wagon starting in the 1950s with his distinctive red and yellow billboards that motorists could seemingly spot a mile away. He adopted "Relax, Refresh, and Refuel" with the idea of creating a simple roadside respite where travelers could take a break and spend a little money.

It worked, and his billboards began to pull customers in by the thousands, our signs becoming as much a part of our brand as our stores and candy. My grandfather attributed his success to a combination of the massive use of Stuckey's familiar red and yellow billboards and a knack for picking locations that paid off. He would joke that those billboards, not candy, were the real secret of his success, and he kept more inventory in billboards than candy. His philosophy was "Tell 'em, and keep tellin' 'em 'til you're sellin' 'em." Another favorite saying was, "Early to bed, early to rise; work like hell and advertise." This derivation of the *Old Farmer's Almanac* quote has been attributed to William Scholl, founder of Dr. Scholl's foot care company, media mogul Ted Turner, and others. Regardless of its source, it was oft repeated by my grandfather, and one I always associate with him. It summarized his philosophy that advertising was at the crux of any successful business. And for a business that resided on America's highways, advertising meant billboards.

Stuckey's had an almost near-total dependence on billboard advertising between 1945 and 1965, with more than 4,000 billboards promoting more than 350 stores across the country. By 1962, we had close to 3,000 10' x 30' signs lining all twelve major highways leading into Florida. "We've got so many signs," my grandfather once told an interviewer, "that sometimes we forget where one is."

At its peak, Stuckey's Corporation had a division called "Signs & Plastics of Georgia, Inc." that occupied a forty-thousand-square-foot manufacturing plant and employed thirty-five persons. The venture manufactured and molded plastic merchandising signs and displays and had four departments: Designing, Molding, Fabricating, and Erecting. The billboards cost about $250 each. As they would sometimes fall hazard to farmers stealing them to build pigpens and patch their barns or hunters shooting out the *e* for target practice, the company added a Maintenance division. It cost $100,000 to employ a full-time work crew to erect and repair the Stuckey's billboards that dotted America's highways.

Credit: Stuckey's Archives

Publicity still of my grandfather next to one of his billboards
in Eastman, GA. At our peak, 4,000 of Stuckey's familiar
red and yellow billboards covered the nation's highways.

Photographer John Margolies, the renowned chronicler
of roadside ephemera, preserved on film the vanishing culture of mid-century America: diners shaped like coffeepots,
gas stations resembling castles, and giant fiberglass pink
elephants advertising souvenir stands. Of the thousands
of color images he shot with his 35-millimeter Canon FT,
Margolies's only photograph of a Stuckey's is, fittingly, a
billboard.

Credit: John Margolies

John Margolies was one of the most prolific and celebrated photographers of roadside America. His book *The End of the Road: Vanishing Highway Architecture in America* warned about modern structures threatening the vernacular architecture that defined road trip culture. His collection at the Library of Congress includes this image taken on Route 17 outside Waycross, GA, in 1979.

Taken outside Waycross, Georgia, the image reflects how billboards were as much a part of roadside iconography—and our brand—as the buildings themselves. Many regarded the garish colors and hokey sayings dotting the landscape as lowbrow, but Margolies viewed them as art worthy of hanging in a museum or gallery. "My parents' generation thought it was the ugliest stuff in the world," Margolies told a reporter in 2015, a year before his death. "I like places where everything was screaming for attention: 'Look at me. Look at me.'"

Like Margolies, my grandfather embraced the gaudiness and persistence of billboard advertising with gusto. They'd exclaim, "Eat Here and Get Gas," "Pecan Log Rolls: 4 for $1 with Gas Fill Up," "New Crop Pecans," and "Breakfast

Special: 99 Cents." He would sometimes start placing them 150 miles from the stores, then 50, up to 1,000 feet, and "Exit NOW!" It'd drive people crazy, but they'd stop anyway.

The advertising campaign worked. By 1960, there were approximately 160 stores throughout the Southeast and up the Eastern Seaboard as highway travel continued to boom. For a while in the 1960s, Stuckey's was opening an average of one store per week, and franchises were making $50,000 to $150,000 per year. The plant in Eastman was shipping 50 tons of candy biweekly to stores, and tourists were offered 54 varieties of candy, plus pecans, jellies, hams, and souvenirs. Stuckey's expanded to the fundraising and catalog business.

Unfortunately, despite their effectiveness, Stuckey's and other billboards started to decline with the passage of the Highway Beautification Act in 1965, a pet project of Lady Bird Johnson, who advocated for scenic enhancements of the nation's highways. While planting wildflowers and cleaning trash were welcome improvements, the First Lady also pushed for restrictions on and removal of billboards, a move that was crushing to businesses like ours. Billboards were our wayfinders before GPS navigation systems and Google Earth maps. Without them, we risked customers passing us by, spotting our distinctive blue roofs too late to make the exit. One Stuckey's manager commented that "Lady Bird Johnson beautified some people right out of business."

One story during this time that's become the stuff of Stuckey family legend is when my father, then a member of Congress, was invited to bring his family to a White House costume party hosted by President Johnson. My mother, usually a model of the tactful political spouse, was none too pleased with Lady Bird's overzealous efforts. Freeway flowers were one thing. But striking a blow at our livelihood was another matter altogether. This meddling in our family's business had awakened the political activist in my mother, more accustomed to bridge games and teas than sign waving at protests. My mother saw the White House affair as an opportunity to exercise her First Amendment rights. She sewed a costume that looked like a pecan log roll and made one of my older brothers, Scott, wear it to the event. To complete the outfit, she made a sign that looked like a Stuckey's billboard that read:

> Oh Daddy to your billboards I'm true.
> But Lady Bird has me all in a stew
> Keeping America Beautiful sure is wise,
> But we all need to advertise.
> Can't I have my candy and eat it too?

All the other boys came to the party as Speed Racer and Superman. Scott never forgave my mother for the humiliation. While this act of protest failed to end Mrs. Johnson's war on billboards, it did succeed in showing that Stuckey's will stop at nothing to save our business—even going to the White House dressed as a pecan log roll.

Chapter 13

FINDING MY VOICE

There is one reason why Bigdaddy was successful. He believed in himself. So much of his story I could replicate in my own life: a willingness to embrace change, hard work ethic, building community. But I couldn't find that inner confidence from reading his papers. That's something that only comes from within. When I first bought Stuckey's, I spent money I didn't have on consultants instead of figuring things out for myself like my grandfather had. They were smart and talented, but their monthly invoices caused constant stress. I also paid social media influencers to rep our brand. Being in my fifties, I didn't think I had the looks or persona that would garner followers. But these influencers knew nothing of our brand. All I got for my money were inauthentic posts labeled "paid promotion." In a year, I'd blown through my meager consulting budget. My biggest accomplishment at that point was having read through my grandfather's papers. I had a thorough understanding of his story. But I didn't know my own.

Out of money but not without resources, I turned to how-to books and YouTube videos to school me on marketing. I devoured Seth Godin and binge-watched GaryVee videos, among others. I loved Godin's purple cow analogy, that your product has to be remarkable to stand out, and GaryVee's infectious energy. But how to translate their ideas into my own brand while still respecting my grandfather's legacy put me in a slump.

Then I stumbled upon an amazing concept that put a name to what my grandfather did so well and naturally: word-of-mouth marketing. I learned about it from an online video featuring Ted Wright who was discussing his book *Fizz: Harness the Power of Word of Mouth Marketing to Drive Brand Growth*. I bought Ted's book and read it, underlining key passages, and filling the margins with notes. His was a bootstrap guide on connecting with customers and building a brand with sticking power.

Ted, who founded a firm called Fizz, was the architect of several major brand comebacks, most notably Pabst Blue Ribbon in the early 2000s. He spelled out for entrepreneurs like me how to apply his methods, for the mere cost of a book instead of pricey consultants. Amazingly, word-of-mouth marketing has been around for about 3,500 years. I read that humans have been sharing stories that they find entertaining and useful with others since cave drawings and hieroglyphics. When those stories are about products—whether it's an earthen vase made by a craftsman in ancient Egypt or a pecan log roll made by Stuckey's—the way to make them more shareable is the same. This was what my grandfather had done fifty years ago. This marketing method could link Stuckey's past with our present. I read on.

Consumers are more likely to buy (40 percent, in fact) because it was recommended by a trusted source. It can be Ramses in the Cairo marketplace in 30 BC gushing over which stall offers the best dates or a mom at the Piggly Wiggly in the 1960s telling her friend how her family pulled over at Stuckey's on vacation and loved the pecan log rolls—the method is unchanged. I can use these same tactics today, without having to pay social media influencers with their millions of followers. The secret is simple: Real conversations between friends, family members, and colleagues are what stick. There is a catch, of course. It may be free, but it requires hard work, consistency, and patience.

A word-of-mouth strategy required that I post daily on all social media platforms with stories worth sharing. That meant, according to Ted's book, it needed to have three elements, neatly summed up in the acronym AIR: Authentic, Interesting, and Relevant. First, it must be real. That doesn't mean that every detail must be included. Don't overshare. Nobody outside close family and friends needs to know the details of your hernia operation. Tease out the parts of what happened to make your point; leave the rest out. Second, it's got to be engaging. I sit at my desk a lot answering emails, but who will stop scrolling to read a post about daily drudgery? Pretend you're at a cocktail party wanting to make a good impression, and don't talk about the weather. Say something that will leave an impression. Finally, it must be relevant. The post is not about you, it's about your reader. Target who your customer is and the audience you want to attract. Tell a story that will be useful or informative to them. Earning your way into conversations like this makes your brand ten times more believable and a hundred times more likely to bring people to try your product.

This is what Bigdaddy was doing, only billboards were his Facebook and print ads were his Instagram. I'm replicating that—albeit in the modern world of TikTok and big data—but still focused on the core goal of getting folks to talk about our brand. And, most importantly, I was learning to do it in my own voice, not his.

Ultimately, though, it's about sales. Look at all the brands that have experienced mega growth, from Dot's Pretzels to Audi to Apple. They've all had the same formula where conversation leads the way. But if the conversation isn't leading to sales, then it's a waste of time. Our goal, Ted summarized, is to sell more pecans to more people for more money. Creating meaningful conversations about our brand is the best way to make that happen.

Of course, this is easier said than done and takes practice, practice, practice. But social media is a great training ground. Where else can you test out a new marketing idea for free at the click of a button? I started experimenting with different posts, steering clear of the usual blah text and pivoting to storytelling. Fortunately, I had no shortage of that.

Armed with the marketing know-how I'd gained from

Ted's book, I began sharing my story daily. But I was still struggling to find my voice. I needed help.

I reached out to Ted on LinkedIn and gushed about what a fangirl I was. As luck would have it, Ted had a soft spot for Stuckey's. The generations of customers who had warm memories of our stores was the gift that kept on giving. Turns out that Ted's grandfather was a civil rights lawyer who worked with Martin Luther King and the Southern Christian Leadership Conference. When they needed a white lawyer to bail out someone in the movement who'd been arrested for civil disobedience, Ted's grandfather was who they often called. Since Stuckey's was one of the few establishments on the highway that was never segregated, he insisted that they always stop there. I have our grandfathers to thank for Ted responding to my message.

Another fortunate circumstance is that Ted's office in Decatur was only a few miles from where I lived in Atlanta. With Ted's client base including giants like JetBlue, AT&T, Bissell, Intuit, and more, I was punching above my weight. But he graciously offered an hour of time with him and his team to strategize about the Stuckey's brand. I left with a notepad filled with notes and lots of ideas.

That led to regular calls with Ted, introducing him to R.G., and asking him to join our board of directors. The board has mostly been a carryover from the days when a Stuckey's board seat meant something, but R.G. and I had kept it going. We realized the value of recruiting experts to advise us on a formal basis. Ted's marketing and financial acumen were a welcome addition to the team we were building.

Our first board meeting with Ted was a doozy. We had a full agenda of finances, production, and staffing. But these discussion items were all hijacked by what defined and guided it all: our brand voice. What had been a perfunctory bullet point to review and approve, our pre-drafted mission statement (which I recall was something ordinary like "to provide superior product and service") became the subject of an existential debate about our very being.

Like a scene from *12 Angry Men*, albeit with a couple of good women in the mix, we were divided into two camps, each persuading the other of its logic. On one side was "Team Pecan," arguing that the Stuckey's brand was all about pecan snacks and candies.

On the other side of the table sat Ted and I on "Team Road Trip." We agreed with the central premise: Yes, Stuckey's makes the most delicious pecan snacks and confections you'll find anywhere. But that's what we do, not who we are. A brand identity is more than how you make stuff—that's a recipe. It's how we make people feel. A few folks may recall our pecan log rolls. However, 99 percent of the stories others share with me about Stuckey's are about one thing: the road trip. You need an emotional hook to sell a product, and let's face it, it's hard to have a personal connection to a pecan log roll.

What the road trip folks talked to me about wasn't simply getting in their cars and going from one place to the next, but the whole experience. Those collective memories of playing license plate bingo with your siblings, singing end-less refrains of "Seasons in the Sun" in the back seat, dad threatening, "Don't make me pull over," and mom packing picnic sandwiches when all you wanted was fast food burgers and fries. That's an experience. That's Stuckey's.

The road trip symbolizes independence and choice—where we want to go and what we want to do—attributes that are uniquely American. From Jack Kerouac's jazz beat musings to the Eagles taking it easy on a corner in Winslow, Arizona, it is embedded in our psyche. The reason that we as Americans are valuing freedom now especially is that there is so much we can't control anymore—the pandemic, climate change, the economy—yet they are impacting our daily lives. We're craving less stressful times when we're in charge, like my brother and I ruling our backseat kingdom. On the road, you can control speed, direction, what's on the radio, snacks, and more. As Ted told me once, "People are glomming onto the road trip in the same way that people glommed onto 'Calgon, take me away' in the '70s." It's an easy, affordable escape, and we love it.

My grandfather innately understood this in how he created an experience. Stuckey's was a break from the sameness of the highway, a safe place where all were welcome. The billboards advertising gas and food every five miles, starting two states away, reminding you that a friend was waiting to greet you if you'd just pull over for a visit. The talking birds, date shakes, salted peanuts, cowboy hats, and fishing lures, all there to remind folks that they weren't at a nondescript exit but an interesting place like Winslow,

Arizona; Mappsville, Virginia; Winnie, Texas; or Milton, Florida. This is the America you can't see thirty thousand feet above the air in a plane. The diners where the coffee is always hot and the waitresses call you "honey," the mom-and-pop trading posts, the llama petting zoos next to gas stations. I'll take that over a bag of peanuts and a complimentary beverage any day.

Ted explained this to the other board members and won them over, one by one. The critical and practical factor for me was a question Ted posed: "What can you tell a story about?" While I can certainly come up with vignettes about the pecan, it's limiting. By contrast, there are literally miles of possibility when it comes to storylines about the road trip. In short, the road trip is full of AIR. It's a real-life adventure full of fun that everyone can identify with on a personal level.

Whether they buy our products at a grocery store in Cleveland doing their weekly shopping or at South of the Border on a family vacation, the connection that Stuckey's has with taking a road trip should still be present. "It's like Corona," Ted explained (the beer, not the virus) in a *New York Times* article on our comeback that appeared on June 13, 2022. "Their brand is all about the beach. So, no matter where you are, folks drinking a Corona get the sensation of being somewhere warm and tropical."

Stuckey's is on a mission to bring back what the road trip stands for, that feeling of freedom and exploration that is uniquely American. We want our customers to identify with that emotion when they see our pecan snacks on the nut aisle

or at one of the few remaining Stuckey's stores still in operation. Reviving a brand and introducing it to a new generation
of customers takes years, especially if you are doing it the
old-fashioned way with word-of-mouth marketing. But we're
willing to roll up our sleeves and do the hard work it takes to
bring Stuckey's back to life, one pecan log roll and one shared
story at a time.

Chapter 14

CELEBRATING FAILURE

S tuckey's history is full of mishaps and missed opportunities. Rather than sweeping aside these setbacks, I choose to celebrate them. My grandfather had that unique trait possessed by most successful entrepreneurs: a willingness to fail. While it's human nature to brag about what we get right, failure is an incredible teacher and makes two of his stories of defeat worth sharing. The first proves that sticking to what you do best is often best. The other is an embarrassing misstep involving one of the world's most successful franchises.

Bigdaddy's first blunder dates back to 1960 when he ventured into the hotel business. It seemed to make sense—hotels were a natural extension of the Stuckey's hospitality brand. Our stores were already offering two of the essential needs of every highway traveler—gas and food—plus, he had prime real estate along the nation's exits. Adding lodging would complete the Stuckey's road trip experience.

He christened his new brand the "Stuckey's Carriage Inn" and mimicked the brightly colored architecture of other chains of the day, such as Holiday Inn and Howard Johnson's. His hotels had bold pinnacle-topped pyramid roofs, tiled flooring, and neon signage. The mix of glass, steel, and concrete building materials was like other mid-century modern motels of the 1960s. The Carriage Inn represented an affordable elegance, offering a family restaurant, pool surrounded by a courtyard, and, of course, a gift shop.

The first Carriage Inn was built in 1960 in Eastman, about a mile down the road from the candy plant. For over thirty years, weary travelers would stay the night on their way to and from Florida and other points north and south. It was shuttered in the 1980s and lay in disrepair for almost two decades before being torn down in 1996. Locals scavenged for parts, the roof reportedly now resting in a field outside of town.

The other locations met similar fates. The second inn, built a year later, surpassed the first as a tourist destination on Jekyll Island, Georgia. Owned by my father, it was one of the premier hotels on the Island, proclaiming itself as a "yearround resort." A brochure highlighted its friendly personnel and many amenities: 106 rooms where "deep carpeted luxury" awaited, an 18-hole golf course "fashioned out of the virgin landscape by the sea," "fast tennis courts," and—the inspired finishing touch—a Georgia-shaped pool where visitors could take a refreshing dip. Everyone from doctors to newlyweds flocked to the resort.

The motel was a hit, except for one minor flaw: There was no alcohol. Since its founding as a state-run park in 1947, Jekyll Island had been dry. Governor Vandiver went so far as to proclaim to the *Brunswick News* in 1959 that no state license to sell alcohol would be granted on the island as long as he was governor. It wasn't until a local referendum legalizing alcohol was passed in 1971 that cocktail lounges were finally added to the resorts on Jekyll. Sadly, it was too late to save the Carriage Inn. The building found new life as different establishments, at one point being remodeled as a Ramada Inn, until its demolition in 2005. The site now hosts a Marriott Courtyard Inn, with nothing remaining of its original occupants, sadly not even the spectacular swimming pool.

The longest-running Stuckey's Carriage Inn was at the unlikely location of Altamont, Illinois. It had an L-shaped, two-story design, with guest room doors painted in sherbet shades of lime, orange, and lemon. The courtyard pool was lined with lounge chairs and bright umbrellas. Once considered "one of the most elegant motels in south central Illinois," the inn hosted the local annual Schuetzenfest during its heyday. A sharp contrast to its alcohol-free sister motel on the Georgia coast, the Altamont location served up classic German beer on tap, along with bratwurst and sauerkraut. One of my favorite images of Stuckey's is a postcard from the Schuetzenfest featuring stein-holding Stuckey's employees dressed in dirndls and lederhosen. Ultimately, though, even an Octoberfest couldn't save this last holdout of the Stuckey's hotel experiment.

Credit: Stuckey's Archives

This remains one of my favorite Stuckey's photos. The Schutezenfest in Altamamont, IL, taken at the Stuckey's Carriage Inn.

It's hard to predict if a spinoff business will add to or detract from your brand. Without the vertically integrated supply chain that Bigdaddy had for his stores, my guess is that the finances and logistics weren't robust enough to take on the complexities of hotel operations.

Perhaps because the motels didn't catch on like the stores, there is limited information on why the Stuckey's Carriage Inn concept failed. However, what is evident is that the setback did not deter my grandfather. The fact that only a few Carriage Inns were built suggests that he simply pivoted, opting to cut his losses and move on to more profitable ventures.

Business school journals are replete with case studies cautioning businesses not to diversify beyond their core competency. Examples include successful brands like Coca-Cola's ill-fated wine venture and *Cosmopolitan* magazine's yogurt brand, and even savvy entrepreneur Richard Branson suffered a defeat when his Virgin Cola fizzled.

The fact that he tried, stumbled, and kept moving forward is why my grandfather was ultimately successful. We learn from failure as much, if not more, than from success. Sometimes sticking with what you know—and doing that exceptionally well—is the most effective strategy. My grandfather's Carriage Inn venture proves that as well as any case study.

The biggest regrets are often the risks not taken. That certainly is true of the other failure lesson from my grandfather. And that's the time he turned down the chance to partner with Truett Cathy, founder of Chick-fil-A.

First started in Hapeville, Georgia, in 1946, the popular restaurant chain began as the Dwarf Grill, a popular lunch place for workers at the nearby Ford Assembly Plant. Fifteen years later, Cathy developed a method for pressure frying a quick-service chicken sandwich. As the company's trademark slogan would later boast, "We Didn't Invent the Chicken, Just the Chicken Sandwich." Cathy's recipe became their signature dish.

The company's initial expansion strategy from 1964 to 1967 was to license their chicken sandwich to other restaurants, including Waffle House. It was during this time that Truett and his son Dan made the two-hour trek to Eastman to pitch a licensing deal to Stuckey's. They donned aprons and grilled up their now famous chicken sandwiches in the test kitchen. Bigdaddy pronounced it delicious. But he passed. His rationale is lost to time. Perhaps he didn't want to detract from the Stuckey's brand. Or perhaps he just made a bad decision.

Whatever the reason, the world knows the rest of the story. Chick-fil-A expanded to suburban malls in 1967, followed by freestanding locations in the 1980s. Today, the company (now run by Dan's son Andrew Cathy) has more than 2,900 locations nationwide and is consistently ranked along with McDonald's and Taco Bell as among the most profitable fast-food chains.

That my grandfather should've considered giving a promising entrepreneur a shot is an obvious lesson here. But, deeper than that, Cathy's proposal offered a solution to one of Stuckey's persistent challenges. Our stores have long struggled to make their food service operation more profitable, with labor costs eating into our margins. And, while the homemade pimento cheese sandwiches, banana shakes, and homemade pies that store managers whipped up were wonderful, these were costly to make. Here was an affordable and tasty option that would have been unique among the roadside offerings of the day. It was a misstep on many levels, and one that the passage of time has made all too glaring.

As a postscript to this story, eighteen years later, I was invited to deliver remarks to a gathering of young entrepreneurs at Trilith Studios sponsored by Chick-fil-A. Unbeknownst to me until I arrived, Dan Cathy, whose family trust owns Trilith, was not only in attendance but had requested to introduce me. I had grown up hearing about how Bigdaddy passed on Chick-fil-A, never knowing if it was true or the stuff of family lore. With Dan Cathy seated in the front row, I skipped my prepared remarks and told the audience the story of my grandfather's failure. I looked down at Mr. Cathy and asked, "Did this really happen?" The former CEO of one of the world's most successful franchises nodded his head. "I'm sorry," I said with a half grin, tossing my hands up in the air. Cathy didn't skip a beat. "It's OK," he shot back with a forgiving smile. "We did all right," as the crowd laughed and applauded. Failure isn't something to be revealed in hushed tones but shared with a roomful of strangers—even if that room includes one of the wealthiest men in the world. My grandfather unwittingly taught me that, and I'm grateful.

Chapter 15

GHOST STORES

I get dozens of them every month—posts and emails from Stuckey's fans sending me images of closed Stuckey's from all over the country. I call them "ghost stores," some shuttered, some repurposed, but most still standing. Of our 368 stores that once populated America's highways, only thirteen are still operating as Stuckey's. That leaves hundreds that remain, like sturdy oak trees refusing to budge from their rightful spot. New coats of paint and signage attempt to disguise their prior lives, but the tell-tale signs betray their true identity: sloped roof, teal paint, zig zag car canopy, etc. Places like Exit 231 off I-90 in Tokio, Washington, where a former Stuckey's now sells a different kind of roll as a cannabis shop. Or the old Stuckey's in Baker, California, that became Arne's Royal Hawaiian Motel and was recently put on the auction block. There's an old location in Quartzsite,

Arizona, next door to where *Nomadland* was filmed, that today is a meat-and-three, murals of the desert painted on its sides instead of the dripping oranges of my grandfather's day.

Credit: Holly Aguirre

Ghost Stores: I always stop whenever I see stores that used to be a Stuckey's. I love it when they find new lives supporting other small businesses, like this meat-and-three restaurant in Quartzsite, NM.

One of my favorites is in Springfield, Illinois, along Route 66. Owner Ron Metzger has transformed the Stuckey's into the Motorheads Bar and Grill. It's an epicenter of the community, hosting corporate events, classic car shows, motorcycle meetups, and concerts on weekends.

The interior is chock-full of roadside Americana collectibles, including one of the few original Stuckey's billboards still around. Best of all, Ron has saved the arched cathedral ceiling, the chandeliers still miraculously intact. The "aha" moment my grandfather loved so much is thankfully still there.

Credit: Justin L. Fowler, *The State Journal-Register*

My favorite former Stuckey's is the Motorheads Bar & Grill,
where owner, Ron Metzger, has beautifully restored the architecture
(including the classic arched ceiling) of the building.
Motorheads has the only original billboard that's been restored.

I recently got kicked out of one ghost store in Yulee, Florida. I was filming a TikTok video and joked about what I would say to the building if it were human. "I am your mother," I cried in a deep tone, riffing on the Star Wars scene where Darth Vader reveals who he is. I broke into my own voice, "You are adopted, young Road Walker. Come back to me." An irate clerk at the Florida Citrus Center ran out. "Cut that off NOW," he yelled as I hoped in my car and sped off.

Not to make this a tell-all confessional, but I have a

history of minor acts of rebellion like this. A few years ago, while driving through Tennessee with my best friend, Holly Aguirre, I begged her to pull over at the former Stuckey's in Pelham where I had gone as a kid on family vacations.

Credit: Holly Aguirre

Scene of the Crime: Me at the abandoned Pelham, TN, Stuckey's moments before my best friend and I repatriated former Stuckey's memorabilia from the inside.

Holly and I have taken countless road trips together, starting when we were students at UGA going to see our favorite bands on tour like R.E.M. and Love Tractor. Holly is used to me insisting we stop at every ghost store; she was already signaling to exit and merging onto the off-ramp. What we saw as we pulled into the parking lot was heartbreaking: peeling paint, gas pumps beyond repair, trash everywhere. It had become a homeless encampment, with sleeping bags and drug paraphernalia littered inside over the once spotless checkerboard floors. The side door was cracked ajar—"An open invitation to explore!" Holly announced as if there were a welcome mat. The place was as hot as a sauna and reeked of piss. I flashed a cell phone light against the wall. It was surreal. The framed prints of pecan log rolls, divinity, and pralines still hung where I remembered them as a kid. Everything else was in frightening disarray, but those prints needed to be saved. Holly gave me a side glance, and we silently knew what we had to do. We snatched the prints off the walls, rushed outside, and got into the getaway car. Speeding off with the air conditioning and radio blaring, we high-fived one another. "I don't think of this as theft," Holly rationalized. "It's repatriation. We are restoring that property to its rightful owner." And that is exactly what we did. The prints now hang on the walls of the Stuckey's in Summerton, South Carolina, the oldest one of our stores still operating. The prints are home where they belong.

These ghost stores are like flashing warning signs: "Danger! Proceed at your own risk if you sell your company." These stores are reminders of what can happen when you lose control. It can make you wealthy. It can also destroy everything you built.

Ours is not the only cautionary tale from that era. Look at what happened to Howard Johnson's. Their history is the most poignant, as they were fellow travelers on America's highways in the 1960s and '70s. With over 1,000 locations—compared to Stuckey's 368—Howard Johnson's downfall was an even greater nosedive. Having always felt a personal kinship with their brand, the death of the last Howard Johnson's restaurant inspired me to pen this obituary on June 2, 2022:

Today I mourn the death of a business icon just as I would a person. It's emotional for those of us who understand the grit and vision that go into building a company from nothing, only to see it perish.

Growing up in the '70s, pulling over in our woodie station wagon at Howard Johnson's for fried clam strips & hot dogs grilled in butter was as much a mainstay of our family vacations as stopping at Stuckey's. Back then, Howard Johnson's was the largest restaurant chain in the U.S., with sales surpassing McDonald's, KFC, and Burger King combined. Now all that is left are fading orange roofs on the nation's highways, ghosts of vacations long past.

What happened to the restaurant that was a road trip staple for generations? Like my grandfather, Howard Deering Johnson built his highway empire from nothing and sold out to corporate America for a lot of money. What followed, like with Stuckey's, was a series of corporate owners that gradually sold off the chain's real estate or converted them to other restaurants.

This week, the lone Howard Johnson's that remained in operation, shuttered its doors. The restaurant, located in Lake George, NY, recently placed the property up for lease. "Lake George is officially dead," a fan bemoaned on Facebook, "Cobwebs on the door."

While I mourn the death of all family businesses,

Howard Johnson's has hit me particularly hard. I feel like I've lost a brand brother, their orange roofs synonymous with roadside America as much as Stuckey's blue roofs. The world is a little lonelier this morning knowing that I'm traveling on this comeback journey without HoJo's as my companion. R.I.P., Howard Johnson, thanks for the memories . . . and the orange sherbet.

Chapter 16

DOWNFALL, THEN REBIRTH

W hat happened to Stuckey's?" is a refrain I have heard my whole life. The simple answer is that my grandfather sold out. Yet, the reasons behind that decision were not simple at all. To understand why, you have to know his story.

By the 1960s, Stuckey's was growing along the interstate as fast as kudzu. Bigdaddy wanted the number of his stores to match America's desire for the road trip: stretching as far as the highway horizon. But his business was starting to sputter with the constant push to expand. Even with his vertically integrated operations, pushing west of the Mississippi, a critical demarcation line in his mind, was stretching his resources. Freight costs especially made the move beyond our eastern base expensive.

Lacking the infrastructure and financing to continue the pace, Bigdaddy began merger negotiations with a company that seemed an ideal fit. Pet, Inc., a St. Louis–based dairy products company, had the capital and human resources to open new stores. For its part, Pet saw the acquisition as a key component of its expansion strategy.

Pet was run by Theodore "Ted" Gamble, grandson of the company's founder, Louis Latzer. Their backgrounds could not have been more different. Ted had inherited his company and boasted degrees from Purdue University and Harvard Business. Yet, Ted and my grandfather shared an ambitious desire to prove themselves and became friends.

Pet was best known for its evaporated milk product, but Ted charted a strategy, which began in 1958, to move his family's business beyond the "staid old Pet Milk" to a diversified corporation. He complemented their portfolio with other food-related ventures, including Schrafft's restaurant chain, Reese Foods, and Haussmann store equipment. Most notable of these additions was Whitman's chocolates, famous for its sampler box and a well-established brand. Stuckey's was a natural tie-in to Pet's candy division, along with the restaurant expertise they were gaining with Schrafft's.

A corporate merger is akin to a marriage. The two parties commit to each other with the best of intentions and often much fanfare, dreaming of a lifetime of happiness together. Yet, the statistics bear out that the honeymoon phase is often short-lived. Almost 50 percent of American marriages fail. And the numbers for corporate unions are even more staggering—a whopping 70 to 90 percent of acquisitions fail.

The reasons for the demise of both are similar: unrealistic expectations, lack of communication, a disconnect with each other's values, and more. Ultimately, it can be attributed to simply not being compatible.

Lots of mergers have failed: AOL and Time Warner, Daimler-Benz and Chrysler, Google and Motorola, Kmart and Sears, eBay and Skype—and those are just the more public, epic ones. In my grandfather's era, there was Howard Johnson's restaurants, Baskin-Robbins, and Holiday Inn. By contrast, some of America's most beloved businesses that have stood the test of time have remained in family hands: Chick-fil-A, Waffle House, In-N-Out Burger, to name some of my favorites.

My grandfather's reasons for selling made sense at the time. Pet had the resources Stuckey's needed. To ensure continuity in leadership, Ted agreed to make my grandfather head of the Stuckey's division at Pet and gave him a seat on the Pet board of directors. My grandfather trusted that he'd remain in control of the company he had built. He wasn't letting go, he figured, but rather bringing in more resources.

And let's not overlook that the deal made Bigdaddy a very wealthy man. A survivor of the Great Depression, financial prosperity for himself and his heirs was as important a family legacy as the business he'd built. He was not unlike other great entrepreneurs of his era—Kemmons Wilson, Harlan Sanders, and Howard Johnson—who viewed selling their companies at a large profit as a mark of success.

There is one part of my grandfather's story that is hard

to understand. Why didn't he make his son CEO? My father had a business and law degree from the University of Georgia and worked at Stuckey's for years. He understood the finances, logistics, brand, and culture better than any other candidate. My father even established a subsidiary that ran Stuckey's stores in New Mexico, Arizona, and California. This was his own business that he controlled, and it remained separate from the Pet deal.

Here is the answer I have always been given. My father had political aspirations. In the early 1960s he was laying the groundwork to run for Congress. He wanted the freedom to pursue his own ambitions. And my grandfather was not ready to let go. Bigdaddy planned to stay on as president and chairman of Stuckey's after the merger. My father becoming CEO was simply not part of the deal.

Families are complicated and so is running a business. It's like when I told my father he had to decide if he wanted a daughter or a business partner. I think family should always come first. It may have broken his heart, but my grandfather made the right choice.

So, on December 14, 1964, my grandfather sold Stuckey's to Pet, Inc. for $15 million, almost $145 million in today's dollars. The merger included the Stuckey candy factory, the right to expand new Stuckey's stores, and the Texaco gasoline proceeds, according to the *New York Times* on September 2, 1964. Pet did not acquire my father's western stores at this point. However, since Pet supplied the gas and candy for Stuckey's, there was a profit-sharing split between the two entities. The move proved an immediate success, as Pet Milk gained 1½ points on the New York Stock Exchange on the day the deal was closed.

Three years later, in 1966, Pet's total ownership of Stuckey's was solidified when my dad was elected to Congress. He and his partners sold their shares of Stuckey's Stores, Inc. to Pet. During the remainder of the decade, with my grandfather still largely involved and benefitting from the resources Pet offered, Stuckey's stores grew in number from 160 to 350 in 45 states, spreading as far west as California and as far north as Vermont.

A national advertising campaign was launched during this time, with a popular jingle that went, "Every trip's a pleasure trip when you stop at Stuckey's. Father, mother, sister, brother, love to stop at Stuckey's." There was a Highway Happiness promotional board game given to kids free when they went to our stores. The goal was to be the first to reach "Lucky Lake" at the "Last Resort" while passing roadside attractions like "Funny Forest," "Dusty Town," and "Moon Mountain." Players would advance to the next Stuckey's or go backward if they drew an unlucky card reading, "Forgot Suitcase, Return Home."

Despite this initial boom period, the merger with Pet ultimately proved to be a major setback. The leadership and culture at Stuckey's became more corporate. Gone were the days of my grandfather greeting workers personally at the candy plant and driving to check on his stores, replaced by him flying a corporate plane to St. Louis for Pet board meetings. The beginning of the downfall sadly occurred on March 12, 1969, with Ted Gamble's untimely death of a heart attack, at age forty-four. His obituary in the *New York Times* noted his leadership in diversifying Pet, citing that his expansion program initially paid off with sales and earnings tripling from 1958 to 1967. In fact, Gamble devoted 75 percent of his time to new markets and acquisitions in 1964, the year of the Stuckey's merger. However, a reversal in fortunes occurred in 1968, attributed to strikes, a declining market for evaporated milk, and a reluctance to introduce new products. This led to mass layoffs at the corporate headquarters, according to the *Times* account.

With Pet's future uncertain, the management of Stuckey's began to decline. In 1970, without his friend and colleague at the helm and his health faltering, my grandfather took early retirement. I have my own suspicions about how voluntary this was, but history has a way of being kind to the past.

Stuckey's didn't fare well after its founder's unexpected departure. The company that had served as a friendly stop to travelers across America had shrunk to a subsidiary of a corporate behemoth, losing its identity and specialness.

Unfortunately, global events also dealt a crippling blow to Stuckey's at that time: an oil crisis. Triggered by the Arab-Israeli War, Arab members of OPEC (Organization of the Petroleum Exporting Countries) imposed an embargo against the United States in retaliation for President Nixon's decision to support the Israeli military. The move resulted in a ban on petroleum exports and significant cuts in production. This put immense pressure on the already strained U.S. economy that had become increasingly reliant on foreign oil. A spike in gas prices followed: first doubling, then quadrupling and continuing.

Higher prices at the pump meant less cars on the road. The cascade of events followed: Fewer cars meant fewer trips meant fewer businesses. Thousands of places like Stuckey's that catered to motorists—gas stations, convenience stores, and truck stops—were hit equally. Vacations were limited to a three-hundred-mile radius, and roadside tourism—hotels, restaurants, and attractions—suffered.

Watching the evening news dominated by images of cars lined up for blocks at gas stations, my grandfather grew restless in retirement. The passion and purpose he had found in running Stuckey's was missing from his days now filled with traveling the world and entertaining friends. His health declined along with his spirit.

Bigdaddy's story is almost over. As I was writing the closing chapters, my father called me to check on my progress. "I'm almost done," I said, relieved, waiting for congratulations that didn't come. "There's something you need to know," he said, adjusting his hearing aids with a screech in the background. "You have to include how bitter he was at the end. It was awful. Your grandfather was so erratic, he had terrible mood swings. We all suffered with him." I paused, shutting my laptop and my eyes. "That's not how I remember it, and that's not how I want the story to end," I said. "I know," Dad said sadly, "but that's how it did end."

He's right. That is how it ended. It was December 25, 1976, my eleventh birthday. Bigdaddy insisted on the whole family gathering for the first time ever: uncles I did not know and cousins I had never met. His two younger brothers, Frank and Felix, along with their spouses and children. My parents and my siblings, Billy, Stuart, Scott, and Jay, plus Dad's sister, Lynda, and her family. Twenty Stuckeys in all, each of us unsure what to make of this hasty and awkward gathering.

Bigdaddy paced the room, agitated that the photographer was late. He called me to sit with him on the sofa while we waited. "Happy birthday," he said. I thought he'd forgotten, along with most of the others. If you are born on Christmas, you get used to that. "I have a present for you." He eyed me sternly, not at all what I was expecting from a gift-bearing grandfather. "But you have to make a choice." He pulled two envelopes from his coat pocket. "One contains a hundred-dollar bill; the other a hundred shares of stock in Pet." He let that sink in for a minute before asking the question, "Which gift do you want?" I didn't hesitate. I had no clue what stock was. "I want the hundred dollars, Bigdaddy!" I said, figuring in my head how many Barbie dolls I could buy for that much money. He looked so disappointed, "Well, you're a damned fool. I'm giving you the stock because you don't know what's good for you."

The photo taken right after shows Bigdaddy sitting stiffly on the sofa in his living room, looking much older than his sixty-six years. I'm standing right behind him, staring somberly into the camera. Everyone is casually dressed. Everyone, that is, except for Bigdaddy. He is immaculately attired in a nice suit, looking off in the distance, a thin smile on his tired face. Two weeks later, he was dead. For the record, I never got the stock.

Credit: Stuckey Family Photo

Family Photo, December 25, 1976. Bigdaddy and Bigmama
with their grandchildren. This is the last time
I saw my grandfather. He died two weeks later.

Boots drove us to the funeral in my grandparents' Cadillac. The church was packed, a throng of television cameras and reporters outside. It was the first time I realized that my grandfather belonged not just to our family but to our community, that he'd done something extraordinary with his life.

There was an obituary in the *New York Times* with the headline "Built Candy Store into National Chain." The article relayed how he'd started Stuckey's with a $35 loan from his grandmother ("her life savings"), going from house to house buying pecans, opening his first store a few years later. After World War II, the business began to steadily add stores until, by the time of his passing, there were hundreds of Stuckey's stores. Throughout those years, the article read, he awarded franchises to friends and family as the company prospered. He's quoted as saying, "A lot of people in town own interests in the stores. They all profited by it. There are more Cadillacs in Eastman, Georgia, than in any town this size in the South, I reckon." Despite his final bitter months, this quote is a fitting memorial of a lifetime of generosity.

My grandfather's death ushered in the death of his dreams as well. Its visionary founder gone, Stuckey's declined further. In 1979, Pet was acquired in a hostile takeover by Illinois Central, or IC Industries, a Chicago-based railroad conglomerate. After that, only a few new stores were built. And within just a couple of years, IC Industries began to rid their portfolio of Stuckey's, most notably the stores.

The places that had been happy stops for generations of road trippers across America were now being discarded as nothing more than assets on a balance sheet. Road trippers like Truman Capote on a cross-country jaunt with New York socialite C.Z. Guest. Or Sid Vicious getting a chili dog at the Stuckey's in Tennessee when the Sex Pistols were on their 1979 World Tour. Or the actor Rob Lowe, who reminisced on a recent podcast about stopping at Stuckey's as a kid growing up in Ohio. "Stuckey's?" he wondered out loud. "Whatever happened to Stuckey's?" Thousands of customers, famous and not, were treated like they were special, and belonged. For, in the words of my grandfather, "the friendship of the traveler is everything."

The remaining franchise owners, many of whom had been personal friends of my grandfather, became increasingly frustrated with how the chain had fallen. What had once been "the Howard Johnson of the highways," complained one owner, was becoming an embarrassing eyesore. They had a long litany of broken promises, both oral and written, that led to a group of operators threatening legal action.

Wanting to rid their balance sheets of an increasing liability and avoid a costly lawsuit, IC Industries was eager to sell. Fortunately, on May 1, 1985, after a year of negotiations, my father and his partners, Chip Rosencrans and Greg Griffith, bought what remained of Stuckey's. This included the trademark, the franchise system, and the few remaining company-owned stores. Thus ended a seventeen-year period during which the company was not owned by a Stuckey. The former candy plant in Eastman was acquired by Nashville-based Standard Candy, makers of Goo Goo Clusters and King Leo candy sticks. An arrangement was made for Standard to produce the pecan log roll and other candy products for Stuckey's. My father was experienced in retail operations. Given the challenges they faced reviving the brand, it made sense for him and his team to focus on what they did best and outsource the manufacturing.

From its peak of 368, the number of stores was diminished to less than a hundred by the time my father's group stepped in. While no longer the roadside empire it had once been, at least Stuckey's was being run by a Stuckey again.

History is full of stories like ours, visionary founders who grow and sell their businesses. Being trashed by outside owners is sadly not unique either. Where our story diverges from the conventional narrative is that we got our family business back. That doesn't happen every day. In fact, it almost never happens.

At the time he bought Stuckey's, my father reflected in an interview that the move was based 80 percent on emotions and 20 percent on finances. While that may be true, the acquisition fit well within his business model. Dad, Chip, and Greg had been successful in running a company they founded, Interstate Dairy Queen Corporation (IDQC). In what proved to be a brilliant business move, my father approached the CEO of American Dairy Queen in 1976 about expanding the popular soft-serve ice cream to the highway system. While Dairy Queen was ubiquitous in small towns across the country, they were not keeping pace with other restaurant chains that were rapidly populating roadside America. My father had recently decided not to run for re-election to Congress after serving five terms ("that was more than enough of a tour of duty," he later recounted). Dad had spent ten years on the Interstate and Foreign Commerce Committee and chaired a subcommittee on Interstate Commerce and Transportation. Moreover, his years of running store operations for Stuckey's offered firsthand experience in retail operations. Who better to help expand one of America's iconic restaurants to the highway than the son of another American iconic restaurant?

By 1977, IDQC held the rights to franchise Dairy Queen on the interstate highway system for all forty-eight of the continental U.S. states. They built upon their growing franchise locations to align the remaining Stuckey's stores with their Dairy Queens. My father's team modernized Stuckey's look by repainting the teal-colored roofs with vibrant royal blue and updated the logo with an '80s vibe. The stores continued to offer our classic candies and souvenirs while the snack bars were replaced by DQ blizzards, soft-serve ice cream, and Brazier Burgers. As the Texaco deal was sadly long gone at this point, they brokered an agreement with Citgo to provide gasoline for the stores.

"Stuckey's Express" was also launched during this time—a store-within-a-store concept that would complement existing c-store and travel-stop operators' businesses. The Express model created a turnkey operation, with Stuckey's Corporation acting as a direct vendor for Stuckey's signature candy but also hundreds of gifts, souvenirs, and novelties for which our brand had become famous. Store owners would pay a franchise fee and could devote as little as two hundred to five hundred square feet to create a Stuckey's Express within their store.

I was studying French in college during this time, hardly the likely heir to take over the business. But I do remember complaining to my father about the new logo and store design. I loved our classic look that I have always considered to be timeless. But my father understandably wanted to put his own mark on the business, which I respect. It was sad, though, to visit some of those combined stores and see the Dairy Queen section more dominant. We disagree on this point to this day, my father holding firm that Stuckey's had peaked in the '70s and needed to align with the more established Dairy Queen to survive. However, the alignment resulted in more resources for Stuckey's and attracted new customers. My father, like me, had to figure out how to reinvent the brand and restore the company to profitability. He and his partners deserve much credit for saving Stuckey's from extinction.

By 1998, my father's team had more than one hundred locations in twenty-three states, with slightly less than half of these being stand-alone units. The combination with Dairy Queen and the rollout of Stuckey's Express in other, third-party locations kept Stuckey's in business. But IDQC remained the more profitable side of operations, with a sizable infrastructure of staff including two accountants and an in-house franchise lawyer. The Stuckey's Express concept unfortunately proved less reliable than the stand-alone stores, with accounts lost as convenience stores were bought and merged with other, larger corporations. An example of this is the Wilco chain that once adopted the Express model in its stores. They were acquired by Speedway, then Circle K, and Stuckey's was dropped in the succession of owners.

Another by-product of this model was the dilution of the Stuckey's brand. Being housed in other locations, we lost control of the overall store look and management. It became harder for us to dictate whether the bathrooms were kept clean, the shelves were stocked, or a myriad of other issues critical to our customer service. Owners of the original stand-alone stores were sometimes resentful to be competing with other c-stores that now carried Stuckey's products as Express franchises. Finally, with the reduced number of stores, it was harder to make the distribution model—which relied on high volumes to keep pricing low—profitable. With the store numbers down since our peak, making the financing work for our merchandising line was increasingly hard.

During this period, Chip, who served as president of Stuckey's, established a new business channel by marketing Stuckey's-branded pecans to grocery chains like Kroger, Safeway, and others. The challenge he faced was making the venture profitable, as grocery stores forced vendors to keep margins tight, not to mention the additional slotting fees, promotional programs, setup charges, and credits for out-of-code items. As Stuckey's was outsourcing our nuts to a third party, there were also embedded production costs. Without manufacturing in-house, Chip's efforts to market a Stuckey's snack line failed to live up to expectations.

Stuckey's was managed by my father and his team, bolstered by Dairy Queen, which continued to generate much of the revenue, for thirty years. By 2014, with the core team approaching retirement age, they sold IDQC to Berkshire Hathaway. Warren Buffett acquired International Dairy Queen in 1997 and operated it as a wholly owned subsidiary. The interstate component that my father had built was an ideal complement to the DQ operations. Unlike my grandfather, my father's merger deal proved to be a smart move. A decade later, his former Dairy Queen stores are thriving under the ownership and management of Berkshire Hathaway. It's a tribute to my father and his partners' business acumen that their company was acquired by one of the most successful investors of our time. Not surprisingly, the Oracle of Omaha had no interest in the Stuckey's side of their shop, which had fared less well even under my father's leadership.

Credit: Stuckey Family Photo

Dad (W.S. Stuckey Jr.) in front of a painting given to him by a former
Stuckey's billboard painter. You can tell from the design that the artist
excelled at billboards, but the proportions of the car and highway are
off. It now hangs in the Stuckey's plant in Wrens, GA.

My father and his partners profited from the merger
with Berkshire Hathaway and were rewarded for their efforts
with a comfortable and well-deserved retirement. The bulk
of the staff also left to find new jobs with the primary operations now sold. Stuckey's stood alone, with only a couple
of staffers remaining to manage the day-to-day operations.
My father continued as the titular chair of the board, and
·Greg Griffith offered support as needed. They maintained a
small office space in Silver Spring, Maryland, where—almost
a decade later—I would sign the papers to purchase what was
left of the company. The remainder of the staff ran distribution in Eastman, Georgia, with a warehouse manager, office

manager, and three workers. A few sales representatives drove the routes to service the stand-alone stores and Stuckey's Express locations. It was a small yet dedicated team that continued to keep Stuckey's operations afloat.

The following decade was not kind to Stuckey's. What had at its peak been a roadside empire boasting more than 350 stores, a candy plant, a trucking company, a sign company, and a small hotel chain, with a staff of over one thousand, had diminished to less than ten employees in rented facilities. The convenience retail industry was becoming increasingly competitive with chains like Buc-ee's dominating exits with Walmart-sized stores and hundreds of gas pumps, offering everything from BBQ grills to beach umbrellas and an array of branded Beaver snacks featuring their mascot. Lacking funding and resources, Stuckey's was unable to keep up with the times. What remained were sixty-eight locations, only thirteen of which were the original blue-roofed stores. The Stuckey's Express concept had steadily been losing accounts and was struggling to be profitable. By 2019, the financial statements were starting to report a loss.

The period before I acquired Stuckey's shows that a business can't be run like a plane switched to autopilot. Truth be told, you can't fly on autopilot either. It takes a skilled captain to remain at the controls and stay on course. The employees who stuck with us during these uncertain years should be applauded for faithfully keeping operations running.

Much credit is also owed to my father and his team for rescuing Stuckey's from outside ownership. Our comeback story is as much their story as mine and R.G.'s. Had they not been willing to take a chance on the middle grandchild with no business experience by selling me their shares, I wouldn't be cohead of the company today. I am thankful to them for seeing the potential in me that I didn't see in myself.

Chapter 17

CHAIR OF THE BOARD

I t has been over three years since I sat at the rickety card table repurposed as a desk and signed the ownership papers of Stuckey's. So much has happened since then. Our manufacturing plant in Wrens is more streamlined. We are replacing our shelling operations with roasting equipment to focus on what we do best: making the most delicious pecan snacks you have ever tasted. We have been building a team with people smarter than me, like Arleen Poquette, who thrives in the complicated world of brokers and distributors. We have hired new talent like Alina Walls, a financial whiz, who manages our books, and Marcos Thomas, who helps drive sales and build company culture. Ted Wright has now been elevated to partner, owning 10 percent of the company. Together with R.G. and me, we are the three amigos who amazingly reach consensus on decisions thanks to mutual respect and a shared passion for building something lasting. Most importantly, we genuinely like each other.

Credit: Marcos Thomas

Three Amigos: Me with my business partners,
Ted Wright (left) and R.G. Lamar Jr. (right).

My role has shifted in the past few days as I finish this book. I am transitioning to chair of the board and passing the title of CEO to R.G., who is better suited for the role. This is a public acknowledgment of the work he has already been doing. R.G. is brilliant with finances and logistics; he is best suited to managing operations. I have the passion for the Stuckey's brand and love making the pitch for new accounts. Recognizing your strengths and your weaknesses is what makes a good leader. I am happy to create space for R.G. to thrive and devote my energies to what I do best.

This shift in leadership roles was inspired in part by Steve Madden. As a shoe lover who sported his signature "Mary Lou" in the '90s, I have been a fan of the popular fashion designer since early on. Admittedly, Madden served time for stock fraud and money laundering twenty years ago, as depicted in the film *The Wolf of Wall Street*. But flawed humans have always been my heroes. It's his hardships that make his life interesting. Madden is a brilliant designer, and he makes beautiful shoes. That's what he does best. So, Madden transitioned to "creative and design chief" for the company he founded and that bears his name in 2005, and handed the operations over to a CEO more suited to the role. Almost two decades after this unconventional move, Steve Madden Ltd. is churning out profits and fashionable shoes. It's a model that works.

I think my superpower is the same as my father's and my grandfather's: recognizing talent in others and building a team. Having a team frees me up to focus on what I love and what I do best: being the most passionate advocate for Stuckey's you'll find anywhere. I don't need a fancy title like "Chief Storyteller" or "Brand Warrior." Chair of the Board suits me just fine.

I don't know what comes next for Stuckey's, but I do know where we've been. My grandfather's story is always a part of me. If there's one part of his life that I hope others will keep with them as well, it's this: have a sense of purpose. For Bigdaddy, it was "Every Traveler Is a Friend." How he made people feel is why our brand has survived.

His purpose has impacted others in ways he will never

know. I'll give an example. Almost thirty years after Bigdaddy's death, I was facing a tough reelection campaign. I had been representing a comfortable district in the Georgia State House. The demographics were aligned with my own: 96 percent white, affluent, and left leaning. After a tough race to initially win the seat, I cruised easily to victory in later elections. Then everything changed when my district was gerrymandered. The demographics shifted to over 70 percent Black and included neighborhoods that were economically disadvantaged. I was also facing tough opposition from the president of the local NAACP. I thought my chances were slim but decided to put myself up for reelection anyway.

The district included a prominent Black church led by a charismatic and influential preacher. His endorsement was critical to gaining the trust (and votes) of the community. I went to worship at his church. In the middle of the three-hour service, the preacher looked down at me in the front pew. "Sister Stuckey is worshipping with us today," he announced in a melodic tone. "Why doesn't she come up and share some words of inspiration with us?" Everyone turned to me and applauded. I am no stranger to public speaking or Jesus, but I sat frozen. I felt like I was back in Contracts Class as a 1L in law school, totally unprepared to be called on. A woman nudged me and whispered in my ear, "Go on! You'll be fine. Just say 'praise Jesus.' A lot." She looked at me and mouthed the words "a lot" again. So, I went up and preached from the pulpit. I don't remember what I said—other than that I did praise Jesus a lot that morning.

Afterward, I went to meet with the pastor in his study.

I braced myself for the expected letdown, feeling sure he would be endorsing my opponent. He looked me in the eye and said somberly, "I'm going to back you and give you my full support." I was stunned. "Wow," I replied. "I'm humbled and thankful. I guess my words from the pulpit were better than I thought." He laughed. "Oh no, honey, that's not why I'm endorsing you." The preacher stopped and his eyes moistened. "I'm endorsing you because of your grandfather; because people who looked like me, and my family, and my congregation, were always welcomed in your stores." And then he smiled, "You also make some really good pecan log rolls."

That's purpose. It lives on decades after you are buried in the ground and changes lives for the better. Here's another story. I gave a speech in Florida last year and talked about how Stuckey's stores were never segregated. Afterward, a Black man who appeared to be in his sixties came up to me. "I never knew that about Stuckey's," he said. "When I was a kid, and our family took road trips, we only stopped at your stores. We would need to use the restroom and be screaming for Dad to pull over, but he would wait for what seemed like hours to find a Stuckey's." The man looked appreciatively at me for a moment. "I always thought he just loved your pecan log rolls. But now I know why we only pulled over at Stuckey's. It is because it was the one place where we were welcomed." I gave the man a hug, so grateful for his story.

My grandfather sold pecan log rolls, gas, and rubber alligators at Stuckey's stores on America's highways. But that is not what he really did. What he did was treat every traveler as a friend. That is why Stuckey's is alive today, even though most of our stores are shuttered. The stores are not our brand. Our brand is how we have made people feel for generations. That feeling lives on in the pecan snacks and candies we make today and in how we treat everyone who comes in contact with our brand.

It has been more than three years since I began my unexpected journey to revive my family's business. Like I did on my first day in November 2019, I typed "Stuckey's" in the search engine on my computer this morning. But unlike that first day, the top hit thankfully did not start with "Whatever Happened To." While, admittedly, stories about our demise are still there, they rank lower now. Most articles include the word "comeback," which is a misnomer. Stuckey's never left; we've just taken a few detours along our journey. It reminds me of the LL Cool Jay lyric, "Don't call it a comeback. I been here for years." Stuckey's has been patiently waiting for years, like my grandfather's papers, to be rediscovered. We all have the power to reinvent ourselves; we control the narrative of our lives. Our story proves that it is never too late to change the ending. Ours, in fact, is just beginning again.

Acknowledgments

I want to thank my father first and foremost for his countless hours relaying memories of my grandfather as research for this book. While I did my best to be faithful to
history, this is my account of what happened and is no doubt
flawed. Please blame any errors on me and not my father's
memory, which is thankfully as sharp as ever at age eighty-
eight. Much love and gratitude also to my mother for giving
me Bigdaddy's papers, which started this literary journey,
and for teaching me to love reading, especially Flannery
O'Connor.

The Stuckey clan will always be a part of our family business. Thanks to my Aunt Lynda for sharing her recollections,
and to the fourth-generation members who have shown an
interest in the business: Will Stuckey IV, Andrew Stuckey,
and William Putnam. Here's to the next generation who will
hopefully keep our family business journey going.

Thanks also to my friends and advisors who have been

generous with their time and expertise in helping revive Stuckey's, including Vicki Horton, Paul Morris, Michael Coles, Bill Bolling, Lauren Fernandez, Kevin Mobley, Tom Keiser, Jay Bailey, and Steven Berkenfeld.

Much appreciation to the other two of the three amigos who make the Stuckey's comeback possible, R.G. and Ted. And a grateful shout-out to all the Stuckey's employees. You are what gives our company life every day. We also love the town of Wrens, Georgia, and Jefferson County. We are excited to be rebuilding our company as part of your beautiful community.

Much love to my best friend and partner in crime, Holly Aguirre.

Most of all, to my favorite road trip buddies, my children, Robert and Beverly. The title "Mom" is the one that matters most of all.

About the Author

Eric Ellis/EllisImages.com

Stephanie Stuckey is Chair of Stuckey's. She received both her undergraduate and law degrees from the University of Georgia. Stephanie has worked as a trial lawyer, served for fourteen years as a state representative in Georgia, and was Director of Sustainability for Atlanta before purchasing Stuckey's in November of 2019 and assuming the role of CEO. Stephanie's achievements include being named one of the 100 Most Influential Georgians by *Georgia Trend* magazine and a graduate of Leadership Atlanta. When she's not running Stuckey's, Stephanie enjoys traveling by car to explore the back roads of America and pulling over at every boiled peanut stand and the World's Largest Ball of Twine.